Be Bully Free

of related interest

Friendship and Other Weapons
Group Activities to Help Young Girls
Aged 5-11 to Cope with Bullying
Signe Whitson
ISBN 978 1 84905 875 9
eISBN 978 0 85700 540 3

Bully Blocking
Six Secrets to Help Children Deal
with Teasing and Bullying
Evelyn Field
ISBN 978 1 84310 554 1
eISBN 978 1 84642 632 2

The Healthy Coping Colouring Book and Journal
Creative Activities to Help Manage Stress,
Anxiety and Other Big Feelings
Pooky Knightsmith
Illustrated by Emily Hamilton
ISBN 978 1 78592 139 1

What are you staring at?
A Comic About Restorative Justice in Schools
Pete Wallis and Joseph Wilkins
ISBN 978 1 78592 016 5

BE BULLY FREE

*A Hands-On Guide to
How You Can Take Control*

**Michael Panckridge and
Catherine Thornton**

Jessica Kingsley *Publishers*
London and Philadelphia

First published in 2017
by Jessica Kingsley Publishers
73 Collier Street
London N1 9BE, UK
and
400 Market Street, Suite 400
Philadelphia, PA 19106, USA

www.jkp.com

Library of Congress Cataloging in Publication Data
A CIP catalog record for this book is available from the Library of
Congress

British Library Cataloguing in Publication Data
A CIP catalogue record for this book is available from the British
Library

ISBN 978 1 78592 282 4
eISBN 978 1 78450 583 7

Printed and bound in Great Britain

MIX
Paper from
responsible sources
FSC
www.fsc.org   FSC® C013056

Contents

Introduction

You're here. That's good. Really good. You have made a powerful first step to rid your life, or someone else's life, of bullying. Thank you.

Bullying. It's probably more common than you think. Research suggests that between one in four to one in six students are directly affected by bullying at school in any week. Let's round that out to one in five or 20% of school students. That's four to six students from your average-sized classroom of 24 pupils. In primary schools, in secondary schools, in private and Catholic schools, in state schools, in single-sex schools, in co-ed schools, in the city, in the country. Small or large, it doesn't seem to matter. It's there and it's happening.

More frightening still is that over 80% of the students in one of those classrooms are aware of the bullying taking place. They are the bystanders. That's a lot of bystanders. A lot of people who can help. If we can get the people who are standing by and watching to step in - to become 'insteppers' rather than remain bystanders - then we will be on the way to breaking the powerful culture of bullying that exists in so many classrooms, in so many schools.

So why are people bullied? It's a tough question to answer but maybe it goes something like this. There is a kind of social order when people are bunched together, especially groups of kids. Some people may see you as different – hey, maybe you have red hair, or maybe your skin colour is not the most common skin colour in your school, or perhaps you're super brainy at maths. Do you speak in a slightly different way than most others? You're wearing *those* shoes? *OMG, I can't believe she said that.* You get the idea? The bullying that goes on is often an attempt to reaffirm social order. Some people are a little threatened by others who are different so they want to set things straight. They want the order of things to remain stable. Putting someone down is a bully's way of ensuring that they stay on top, that they keep their elevated status in terms of social order. Of course, it's a lot more complex than that and there are all sorts of other reasons why people bully. Sometimes people don't even know they are actually bullying someone. Their behaviour might stem from how they were brought up and relate to role models in their family. It's who they are.

The good news is that there are a number of ways to deal with bullying. Some will suit you better than others, depending on the type of person you are. That's okay. Actually, reading the strategies that accompany each of the scenarios or stories will help you get a better sense of the sort of person you are and therefore what strategies will work.

Dealing with bullying can be tough; it can be painful; it can hurt. It can hurt more than the actual bullying. That's because you're dragging the bullying out of a dark corner and bringing it into the light. And you're bringing yourself into the light also. And that's not an easy thing to do for some people. It would be so much easier just to ignore it, pretend it's not happening.

For some of you it's going to be really hard to do what's required to move beyond the bullying situation. But that's not a reason to not give it a go. By allowing it to continue you are defining yourself as a victim and perhaps setting a tone for yourself that will stay with you forever. You're reading this book so already you're trying to set a different tone. A different you. A stronger, more forthright you. A person better in touch with what you believe in, what you hold strong to. A person willing to stand up for yourself and not tolerate bullying in any form.

One more thing. Sometimes there isn't a happy ending. It's not always going to be hugs and kisses and make up and *everything now is just so perfect.*

In this book you will find dozens of answers and suggestions, examples and ideas, tips and definitions. But the ultimate answer lies with you. The goal of this book is to empower you to stand up and deal with any bullying situation - firmly, confidently, directly and immediately. You won't carry this book in your hip pocket for the rest of your life. But if you take on board the ideas and suggestions and use them with a firm commitment to becoming a stronger, more confident person, then hopefully you'll live each day with purpose, poise and direction.

Now read on and get ready for your world and the world of those around you to be a much better, much happier place...

What Is Bullying?

Bullying is when a person or a group of people continue to pick on another person or group of people to upset or hurt them. The hurt can be physical harm or, by the use of words written or spoken directly or indirectly to the recipient, make them feel sad, hurt, ashamed, rejected or humiliated.

AND WHAT IS NOT BULLYING?

If a one-off argument takes place, this is not normally considered to be bullying, especially if the two people are considered to be of equal power in a social sense.

THE BYSTANDER?

A bystander is someone who is aware of the bullying happening but doesn't intervene to stop the bullying. Away from where the bullying takes place, the bystander might sometimes talk in a helpful manner to the recipient.

AND THE 'INSTEPPER'?

This person steps forward in an active manner and by actions or words attempts to both stop the bullying and support the recipient.

WHAT TYPES OF BULLYING ARE THERE?

There are basically three types of bullying.

1. Overt bullying

This is direct, in-your-face bullying with no computer screens, mobile phones, people or bits of paper in between the bully and the recipient. It can be physical or verbal. Physical bullying can include hitting, kicking, pinching, pushing or damaging the property of someone else. Verbal bullying can include put-downs, racist or homophobic comments, insults, teasing or verbal assault. Sometimes it can even be a facial expression.

2. Covert bullying

This is more subtle and harder to detect. It is not physical, more out of the way and hidden. It is intended to harm someone's social reputation and/or humiliate them. People don't readily acknowledge that it exists because it is out of sight. Some common examples include:

* lying and spreading rumours

* negative facial or physical gestures, menacing or contemptuous looks

* playing nasty jokes to embarrass and humiliate

* mimicking unkindly

* encouraging others to socially exclude someone

* damaging someone's social reputation or social acceptance.

3. Cyberbullying

This is bullying that occurs via information or communication technologies. It can happen via the Internet, text messages, email, social networking sites and other programs where images and text can be stored and/or shared. It can be overt or covert. It can happen at any time, be public or private. The audience to the bullying can be just the recipient or much, much broader.

The Effects of Bullying

People respond to bullying in many ways. Sometimes the response is immediate, such as when being physically bullied. People are obviously aware of the hit, shove or trip. However, in lots of situations, people don't always know they are being bullied until later on. This can happen if the bullying is low key and hidden, such as a series of personal 'put-downs' or social exclusion. In these cases the victim may believe that they are at fault but they don't know what they are doing wrong. It can sometimes take a while for a person to recognise they are being bullied.

Initially bullying affects a person's sense of self. 'I've felt okay before, so why am I starting to feel bad... I really must be a social loser?' or 'What's wrong with me that people are acting like this towards me?' When this happens, victims become very aware of their behaviour and psychologically 'zoom in' to everything they say and do, so as not to stand out in any way. As you can imagine their anxiety thermometer gets very hot.

When a person thinks that it's their behaviour that is 'causing' them to be bullied, the easiest way to deal with it is to 'avoid' - hang out in the library, the toilets or even not come to school in the first place. They feel like a failure and would rather be on their own than 'cause' someone to make or think negative comments about them or attack them physically. Together with avoiding certain situations, when a person 'thinks' about what is happening, they can feel nervous, teary and shaky. Their heart might race when they know they have to walk past the place where the bully usually hangs out. And they may also spend long periods of time on their own, thinking about what they may have done wrong or why people are being so mean. They might even imagine how to get revenge. All this thinking and worrying can certainly make a person feel very tired, which again makes it hard to think clearly and look at options and plan what needs to be done.

It's not hard to imagine that when you're feeling worried and tired your concentration and interest in your schoolwork or hobbies may be affected. Your marks may drop and you don't have the motivation to complete your homework, which will only add to the problem as now you have your teachers and parents on your back! Often all of this leads to sleeping and eating problems. What else needs to go wrong? It's reasonable to say that when a person is being bullied nearly every aspect of their life is affected, especially if it is over a long period of time. Depression and anxiety are common, indeed quite 'normal', responses to being bullied.

The Scenarios and Strategies

The scenarios are all set out in a standard and similar pattern. The story is told, before a variety of strategies are suggested. The strategies written are guidelines only. You might find there are similar strategies in a number of the stories. Hopefully this will be reaffirming for you. The scenarios don't have to be read in any particular order. You can search via the titles in the contents to look for something that might be relevant to you, or browse through them - they're in no particular order, but cover the range of common bullying situations described in the earlier section on types of bullying.

Sometimes the strategy is simply a continuation of the story. Perhaps the character in the story has thought through the situation and taken a course of action that requires no intervention or assistance from someone outside. By their words and/or actions, they are demonstrating a worthwhile strategy to help them resolve the problem.

#1

Simon – who gets an orange thrown at him by a group of boys

Type: Overt – Physical

'Sorry!' I heard one of the boys shout. I looked at the half–eaten orange on the pavement.

My name is Simon Woodfield. I am 11 years old. I really like school. My favourite subjects are maths and science. I work really hard in all my subjects but especially those two. My teachers sometimes give me extra hard work to do at home and sometimes even in class.

In class I like answering the teachers' questions. They're usually quite easy. I don't put my hand up all the time but if no one else knows the answer then the teachers usually ask me and most times I'm able to give them the correct answer.

At recess and lunch I go to the library. Colin, Lindsay and I are working on writing a computer program. It turns a two-dimensional object into a three-dimensional object. Mr Hutton asked me to demonstrate it in class yesterday.

I hooked my laptop up to the oversized screen and showed the class. Mr Hutton asked me some questions about it and so did one of the students in the class.

During lunch while I was walking past the bench near the canteen on my way to the computer lab, I felt a hard thump on my back. I dropped my books. It didn't really hurt much, it just gave me a fright. 'Sorry!' I heard one of the boys shout. I looked at the half-eaten orange on the pavement. I picked up my books and the orange and kept walking, dropping the orange in a nearby bin. I could hear their laughter. I glanced around at them again. They certainly didn't appear to be sorry.

At the end of lunch, it happened again. This time one of the boys 'accidentally' bumped into me.

'Sorry!' he said again, holding his arms up. I managed to not topple over.

'That's okay,' I muttered, feeling totally stupid, because it obviously wasn't okay. This made the boys laugh again. 'What have I done to deserve this?' I wondered, walking quickly to class.

. . . .

Bullying is always hurtful, and when it hurts both emotionally as well as physically it is especially awful. Trying to avoid the bullies is an effective strategy. The plan here is to work on not being where the bullies are, to work out other ways to get to where you are going. Of course this is not always easy. Having some support with you, friends like Colin or Lindsay, will make the trip more comfortable if you do have to be near them.

People say that bullying is an abuse of power, so really work hard at not letting yourself be bullied without your permission. Stand up tall, hold your head up high, and walk away with confidence. Turning the situation into a bit of fun can also act like taking air out of a balloon. Saying something like, 'Probably better that you eat it rather than throw it away,' can help to diffuse the whole situation a little.

Make your point, then smile and keep walking. It might be that if the bullies see that their words and actions are actually not having that much effect they will be more likely to stop their bullying behaviour. It's a hard one, but it's important for the recipient of the bullying to try and not let what they are doing affect how they are feeling about themselves.

There is often no rational reason why bullies target people; the main reason is that they want power and control. It's about them much more than it's about the people they are bullying. But a person's self-esteem can definitely take a hit during these times. At this point, it might be good to consider self-talk. A great first step is to get to know how you talk to yourself. Sometimes we're unaware of the messages we give ourselves. For example, we can be our own worst enemy by telling ourselves that we're not good enough to achieve what we want. Give yourself encouragement and support. Talk to yourself the way you'd talk to your best friend. You can find more information regarding self-talk on page 135.

When thinking about the bullying problem, think less about what's happening and the associated feelings and focus more on what can actually be done about it. For example, a person may be feeling angry and hurt but can still act in a confident and controlled way.

Some people find exercise a really useful thing to do. It can help people feel better about themselves, reduce stress and can also improve thinking.

What's important here is to walk tall and walk away. There are things that can be done that can alter the balance of power and give control back to the recipient of the bullying. Body language is one of these. This is the standing up tall stuff and looking super confident. Doing everything to make it appear that the power and control is not with the bullies, especially on the outside. Walking with purpose and authority, showing a carefree almost uninterested attitude is a strong response. How we look or appear is often how people will see us.

Above all, the recipient needs to demonstrate that they are not in the bullies' power and that the bullies don't have control over them.

Key points to remember

Avoid the bullies by walking a different route.

Keep your friends close to you when you're having to cross paths with the bullies.

Use humour to deflect what they're saying.

Look and behave in a confident way.

Talk to yourself as if you're your own best friend.

#2

Trina – who experiences peer pressure to try something she doesn't want to do

Type: Covert

'Hey, Trina, we've got some cigarettes, are you going to try one?'

I've got a large group of friends, maybe too large! We're one big group. Each weekend we go into town and hang out. It's no big deal - well, it hadn't been, but lately things have been changing a bit. Sometimes we'd do a bit of shopping; mostly we'd just hang out. I liked being with my friends; I liked being part of the group, though I have to admit that sometimes I was a bit uncomfortable with the stuff they talked about. It wasn't so much what they said; it was more how they said it. The last few times the conversation was almost entirely either about cute boys or how slutty other girls looked. Sometimes they were just plain rude about girls that walked by. When they talked like this, I hung back a bit, went a bit quiet. Their talk made me feel a bit mixed up but I didn't want to stand out. But I guess I must have because a couple of weeks ago Neve asked me why I went so quiet and never joined in with them. 'It's only a bit of fun,' she'd said.

Grace, sitting next to her, had rolled her eyes and muttered something under her breath. I felt myself go hot. I thought I'd heard the word 'mummy', but wasn't sure. Maybe I just had to toughen up a bit. Like Neve said, it was probably all pretty harmless really. I just needed to act a bit more streetwise.

The next week though was worse. I was invited to join them but didn't know that they had arranged to meet up with a group of guys. Had they not told me this on purpose? I tried to act cool, though I didn't feel it.

'Hey, Trina, we've got some cigarettes, are you going to try one?' Grace asked.

I said, 'Are you serious?' I guess I spoke the words pretty quickly.

I added, 'No, thanks.'

'Yeah, well, guys, don't worry about her,' Grace said, smiling at the boys. 'She's not really part of our group. We just let her hang around cos we're such nice girls.'

'Do your mummy and daddy know you're actually in town?' one of the boys asked. He was nudging one of his mates. I could feel my face flushing with embarrassment. I muttered something about meeting up with someone and walked away, trying hard to look like I was in total control.

I managed to fight back the tears for the whole 5 km walk home.

. . . .

Often the first step is the hardest. Walking away can be really difficult to do but is a strong statement of attitude and intent. It is a positive choice to remove yourself from the situation and not be involved. It might be considered as simply avoiding, but it's really a lot more than this.

Sometimes it helps to think about friendships and what friendships really are. True friendship is so much more than hanging out with people that you have known since kindergarten or people that live in your street. True friends are people you want to be with and who inspire you to be your best. Friends think of your needs and laugh with you, not at you. What is it that makes a person a true friend?

The following activity will help you identify what it is that makes a friend a true friend.

Think of somebody you admire and are inspired by. It may be a family member, someone famous or someone you know from a local community.

Now, think about what it is you like about this person. Is it their sense of humour? The way they support other people?

Now look at the list of personal qualities below and think of five qualities your person has.

Adventurous	Assertive	Cheerful
Creative	Dependable	Extroverted
Friendly	Generous	Genuine
Impulsive	Loyal	Open-minded
Outgoing	Patient	Positive
Receptive	Reserved	Resilient
Responsible	Sensitive	Sincere
Sociable	Strong	Sympathetic
Tolerant	Understanding	

From the five you've thought of select the two most important qualities that you seek in a friend.

Lastly, try and identify people of your age and who live nearby that have these qualities – the next step is to think about how you could develop a friendship with one or more of these people.

Although it may feel difficult and uncomfortable, sometimes the best decision in these situations is to leave the friendship group. Of course, there may well be temporary feelings of isolation and loneliness, but the bigger picture is that it won't be necessary to keep putting up with the bullying that is happening at the moment.

This could also be a time to look at your level of confidence. Writing down a list of achievements and accomplishments provides you with an opportunity to focus on the positive things you have done and will encourage feelings of pride. Maybe it's success at dancing or acting on stage that's occurred at some point in your life? Perhaps it's time to revisit those passions and rekindle the spark that can bring like-minded people together who all share a love and passion, as well as broaden your network of potential friends.

Key points to remember

Remove yourself from a stressful situation.

Identify values you admire in good friends.

Build on your confidence by writing down your accomplishments and achievements with a view to expanding your interests and increasing your friendship circles.

#3

Marissa – who receives nasty, anonymous texts

Type: Cyber

*They were too gutless to leave any kind
of ID so I had no idea who it was.*

I guess maybe in hindsight it wasn't the smartest thing to do, to go and date Tom, Maddie's ex-boyfriend; but then again, he was an 'ex'. Why shouldn't I? I liked him; he liked me. Maddie was just an online friend. We went to different schools.

Anyway, for a couple of weeks Tom and I had kind of managed to keep it pretty quiet. But then word must have got out as I started to get these random messages on my phone from people I didn't even know. They were too gutless to leave any kind of ID so I had no idea who they were. I started to look twice at my friends at school, holding back a bit to see if they said anything. I didn't want to openly confront them as I didn't want them thinking I was accusing them of something they weren't doing or maybe didn't even know about. I guess I wanted to find out on the quiet if it was any of them. It kind of made me tentative all of a sudden. I really liked Tom but started to doubt whether it was worth the hassle. The text messages continued. Sometimes it was just a word or two. 'Player.' Once it was, 'You're a seagull – scavenging for scraps.' What could I do? As long as I didn't know who was sending the texts I was never going to be able to confront them.

. . . .

There are a number of potential bullying situations that can arise when using mobile phones.

* ★ People can be anonymous.

* ★ They can contact you constantly and at any time of the day or night.

There can be no safe place for anyone unless we each manage when we allow calls to occur and who those calls are from. We own the phone we use and we each need to be the person in charge at all times.

It is also worth looking at who really has the problem. Feel good that you are trying to get on with your own life by following your own inner wisdom. Guess what? It's not you with the problem, it appears to be the bully's issue.

It's perfectly normal for feelings of anxiety to arise when it isn't known who's doing this and they are saying such horrible things. Do you feel like you're beginning to doubt yourself and are less likely to trust your inner judgment?

One good strategy is to just block the sender; they will soon get the message that you are not going to be messed around with and that you have more important things to concentrate on.

Another way to address the situation could be for you to forward the messages on to all of your friends saying something like, 'Hey, look what I am getting. Can you believe someone would stoop so low? What a joke!'

This would certainly send the message out that you think the person is not worth taking seriously. An added benefit would be that your friends also pick up the vibe that anonymous messages are unacceptable. You are modelling assertive actions for your friends.

Key points to remember

Identify who has the problem...it may not be you.

Block the sender.

Turn your phone off when you don't want calls.

It may help to forward the messages on in a lighthearted manner, demonstrating that they're unimportant to you.

#4

Tanisha – who gets the cold shoulder

Type: Covert

Do I walk away, defeated, looking like a loser?

New to the school, I was really keen to make a good start, to learn as much as I could quickly about the kids here and who might be a good group of friends to join. I'd met Meg on Orientation Day, and although we hadn't really communicated much over the holidays, I was hopeful that she might seek me out, at least for the first few days. Maybe I'd get to meet a few of her friends; she seemed like a decent person, so her friends probably would be too.

I saw Meg sitting with a group of girls. Before I could even think what I was doing, I was heading in their direction. I could tell by the easy, confident look that this was a group of popular girls. But I'd made my intentions known, even suspected that Meg had caught a glimpse of me approaching. How would she react?

'Hi!' I said, to Meg's shoulder. She didn't even turn around. She just kept on talking. Maybe she hadn't heard me. 'Meg?' She swung her head around briefly, smiled at me, then turned her back and laughed out loud with the girls at her table. Was she laughing at me? There was no welcome or effort to introduce me. Now that I think about it, it was probably the teachers who had asked, maybe told, Meg to show me around on Orientation Day. Like I said, she'd seemed friendly and was certainly helpful then.

Do I walk away, defeated, looking like a loser? Surely Meg would at least acknowledge me if I sat down. Noticing a gap on the wooden bench on the other side of the table that Meg was sitting on, I moved to join them. But as I placed my lunch bag on the table, one of the girls shifted herself across.

'Sorry, there's really not any room here,' she said, smiling up at me. Feeling embarrassed, I grabbed my lunch bag and headed off. Maybe there's a better spot to hang out, I thought to myself, pretending not to care. But I did care. I cared a lot. It was my first day at school. 'You don't forget your first day at a new school,' Mum had said at the breakfast table this morning. She was sure right about that.

. . . .

Should someone change to be accepted into a group? If someone is feeling like a loser and not part of a group they aspire to be with, they will be overly harsh on themselves. Their self-talk will be negative. They will be putting themselves down all the time.

So it's time to take a step back and think of the bigger picture. The first question to ask is whether you really want to be involved with this group of girls. Thinking about the personalities of each is a good first step. Do they match well with you? Do the things they do and say sit well with you? Are they doing and saying things that you would do and say? What a wonderful opportunity for someone to start questioning their own personal and moral values. And what a great opportunity too to stand up and be the person you want to be.

Often a good way of assessing all this is to put yourself in the shoes of the people who are the recipients of the group's or bully's words and actions. Would you like those words spoken to you? The first few weeks at school, or any new place for that matter, can be a challenge for anyone. But it makes sense to bide your time a little and quietly take stock of the people around you. Good people are there and are certainly worth the wait.

Have a think also about what your priorities are and don't let yourself get sidetracked by those who want to go against you.

Once you've made a firm decision, stick to it. Perhaps chat about it with a friend or someone at home. It can be reassuring to get the support of someone you trust. Yes, I am doing the right thing here.

Sometimes things don't go the way you want or expect. First-up encounters and experiences in new situations can indeed be quite negative. But they won't last.

Being your own best friend is a good place to start. Positive self-talk can help. Hold your head up high, be civil and friendly to everyone around you and get on with each moment of your day with purpose and resolve.

Key points to remember

Be aware of the things you're saying to yourself and about yourself and make sure it's as realistic as possible; be your own best friend (refer to page 135 for more information about positive self-talk).

Learn about perspective and focus on the bigger picture.

Behave in a confident manner – hold your head up high; make eye contact with people you're talking with; smile; stand tall and upright.

#5

John – who receives negative comments on Facebook

Type: Cyber

*On the outside I was the same old
John, but inside I was crumbling.*

It was a crap game and I'd played crap. And that was the end
of it. Or so I thought. I logged on to Facebook that afternoon
and was amazed to see a couple of really negative comments
from a couple of the guys from the team. I guess it was all
just a bit of fun; after all, they were my mates. This was our
second season together. It wasn't as if we'd lost the game
because of my mistakes. The coach had said as much after
the game. Still, it hurt to be called a loser.

So I rang up Jay.

'Mate, it's only a joke,' he laughed. How did I know he was
going to say that? So what do I say? 'Well, it's not a joke to
me.' Or, 'Yeah, fair enough.' Or even, 'Well I guess I am a bit
of a loser. I sure played like one.' We didn't talk much. I spent
the afternoon watching the footy on TV, ignoring my phone
and computer.

But I kept on thinking about the game. I really had made a
couple of clangers. And playing in defence meant it hurt us on

the scoreboard. 'Only a joke,' Jay had said. It sure didn't make me laugh. And so Saturday turned into Sunday and Sunday turned into Monday and still the jibes kept coming. I did my best to laugh it off, even laugh with them. I pretended it was actually funny, that it didn't matter, it was no big deal. But inside it was cutting me up deep. I wasn't sleeping so good, picking and prodding at my food and getting into trouble for not handing in my homework.

On the outside I was the same old John, but inside I was crumbling. The weird thing was, they were still my friends. I kicked the footy with them at lunchtime, sat with them in class; we even talked excitedly about getting some tickets for the first round of football finals.

I had to do something.

. . . .

John needs to think about his friendship with the boys and how they had been hanging out for many years. He really needs to talk to them and let them know how the comments are affecting him. Although he may feel anxious, John needs to take what will appear to be a risk and directly approach them. Yes, he can acknowledge and indeed agree with his friends that he played badly, but the game is over and they need to let it go.

He needs to tell them how he felt about their comments and that he would prefer their support. It might seem like a joke to them, but actually their comments are destructive. He didn't need them to blame him as he was already blaming himself for his bad play.

Directly approaching the people bullying you is an effective way to address the situation, especially if you trust the people and know that they will listen to you. It is quite likely that they have no idea of the effect of their teasing, so in letting them know how you feel you are also educating them about the negative effects of bullying. Sometimes bullying is not an intended outcome. It starts off as playful teasing, but it can escalate and become destructive.

Direct confrontation is best used when you believe that the situation is within your control and you have the emotional strength to address the problem.

Key points to remember

Take control by approaching people to let them know how you feel.

View your approaching them as a chance for them to learn that their behaviour is destructive, and that you might be educating them to help others in future situations.

#6

Danny – who receives untrue emails and written messages

Type: Overt - Verbal

In the space of a couple of days my world
was suddenly spinning out of control.

I didn't actually believe Cam when he said there was a love letter written by me pinned up in the canteen. I thought he was making it up. He wasn't. It was a copy of a fake email with my name at the bottom. I scanned the contents briefly before tearing it down, scrunching it in my fist.

Later in class, I looked at it more closely.

'Hamish - are you okay to meet in our usual spot? Don't tell anyone - I sure won't... x Danny.'

My first thought was to wonder why someone would do that. How many people had seen it? How long had it been up there for? I found out walking home that night.

'Hey, Danny, can we catch up in the usual spot too?' I didn't even know the guy winking at me as I walked out the school gate.

'I didn't write that email. As if I'd put it up in the canteen for everyone to see!' I added, angrily. But that wasn't the worst of it.

'Die faggot,' I read in the first email. I opened another one. 'We'll get to you. Your type is always dealt with in the end.'

I tried calling Hamish a couple of times but he didn't pick up. Surely he wasn't behind this. I didn't go to school the next day. I told my parents I was sick. I must have looked sick because Mum took one look at me and said that was okay. During the day I got more emails. I couldn't help myself. I had to open them.

'Hey, Lover Boy. Are you at home with one of your friends?'

In the space of a couple of days my world was suddenly spinning out of control. What had suddenly caused this? There had been whisperings and the odd crude remark to stir me and bait me, but they'd been one-offs. I'd just tried to ignore them and focus on the good people in my life. Like Hamish. But even he was strangely quiet. The thought of going back to school was suddenly terrifying. But I was going to have to do something.

. . . .

In this situation Danny could take a step back and gain the perspective of the bigger picture.

He could visit various self-help sites to learn more about the effect of bullying and discrimination. For instance, by visiting the Australian Human Rights Commission and Mind Health Connect (see the next page), Danny will learn that equality and freedom from discrimination are fundamental human rights belonging to all people and that people have a right to be granted freedom from discrimination based on their sexual orientation or gender identity. Another site to help understand more about the effects of bullying is ReachOut (see Further Information at the end of the book).

Although beginning to understand the bigger issues, Danny still needs to return to school and deal with his friends.

Certainly he felt 'empowered' by what he had learned, but returning to school was a big hurdle. He didn't think he could cope with any more emails and verbal taunts.

Other strategies Danny might find useful may include blocking the senders of the emails and learning some relaxation strategies to assist him with his feelings of anxiety about coming back to school. Refer to page 132 for more information on relaxation.

The following websites are also helpful:

★ **www.mindhealthconnect.org.au:** This website collates mental health resources and content from the leading health focused organisations in Australia. You can access a range of mental health resources including online programs, fact sheets, audio and video, and online support groups.

★ **www.humanrights.gov.au:** The Australian Human Rights Commission recognises the inherent value of each person, regardless of background, where they live, what they look like, what they think or what they believe.

Their principles are based on dignity, equality and mutual respect, which are shared across cultures, religions and philosophies. They are about all people being treated fairly, treating others fairly and having the ability to make genuine choices in our daily lives.

Key points to remember

Educate yourself about bullying and its effects; this will help you understand that lots of your feelings are normal.

Block the senders of inappropriate emails.

Learn some relaxation techniques to help you with your anxiety.

If the situation doesn't improve, you need to tell a trusted adult.

#7

Melonie – who is excluded from her group

Type: Covert

Jen saying there was no party; Lucy that they're still deciding. I knew one of them was lying.

Looking back, I think it must have probably started soon after my parents separated. I found it hard getting myself organised, living between two homes. Sometimes it was just little things – I'd leave something important for school at one place, sports gear or other clothes. I didn't have two full sets of make-up either.

Although I got on well with each of my parents I found it upsetting that they were making no effort to get on with each other. I mean, of course, they'd separated, but surely they could at least be respectful and kind of nice to each other.

I'd often find myself daydreaming about old times when we were all together. In the middle of class, at the dinner table, playing sport. I found it difficult talking about it to others. Maybe talking about it made it all even more real. At school I started spending more and more time alone, drifting away from my friends. It seemed the right thing to do. They all seemed so happy in comparison to me.

I stayed in touch with them on Facebook though. That was kind of easier. You could pick and choose who you wanted to chat to and how much you wanted to say. Sometimes it was just a few words; then I'd drift away, do a bit of homework, and later come back to check who was on.

A few weeks passed. Things were slowly settling. Dad took me into town and gave me some money to buy some clothes and make-up. That day at school I'd heard that Jen and Lucy were going to be online to plan a party for the following weekend. They'd said they were going to message us. I didn't have much homework. I went for a run, had a long bath and then dinner with Dad. I logged in around nine o'clock. There were no messages for me.

I texted Lucy but got no reply. I sent Sal and Jen messages. I didn't hear from Sal, but Jen replied. She knew nothing about a party. I was sure she'd know. Maybe I was mistaken about the party. I spent half an hour trawling through my friends' pages, looking for clues about a party.

My phone buzzed. It was Lucy.

'Still deciding about party, will let u know, L.'

It was then that I realised I was being left out. Little things that I now recall, looks at school, brief comments from my friends, polite but not with the usual fun and warmth. And then Lucy's text. Jen saying there was no party; Lucy that they're still deciding. I knew one of them was lying.

For the next few days I avoided being anywhere close to my friends. I was feeling sorry for myself and hoping, praying for someone to come up to me, put an arm around me and ask what was wrong. No one did. No one paid me the slightest attention.

I withdrew from the world even further. I was obviously some huge loser. I was a victim of my situation and felt that there was nothing I could do about it, except bring Mum and Dad back together, and that sure wasn't going to happen.

The party was a hit. Everyone was talking about it the following week. I guess it was a good thing I wasn't there...

. . . .

Melonie is being excluded, a covert form of bullying. This means that the bullying is social in nature and hard to detect, as it feels 'hidden'. You know something is not quite right, but you're just not sure what. It can take some time for someone to put the pieces together and recognise that they are being bullied.

As in all types of bullying, the victim feels powerless and, as Melonie has experienced, it feels easier to withdraw into your own world. This type of bullying may lead to a lowering of our immune system, a reduction in our sleep quality, and an increase in feelings of anxiety and depression.

Putting things into perspective may help her situation. Over the past few months Melonie has had a lot to deal with: coming to terms with her parents' separation, having to live between two homes, and coping with her parents not getting along together. This too can impact on moods and behaviour. Is it possible that due to feeling down she started to withdraw from her friends? Perhaps they also felt excluded from her as their friend? Perhaps their rejection of Melonie can be perceived as a sign that Melonie may need counselling support to deal with her acceptance of the separation of her parents and to help her come to terms with how her life has changed.

Sometimes people who have had to experience significant changes in their life develop primary depression. The symptoms are similar to the ones Melonie described, such as withdrawing from friends, problems with concentration and a general feeling of sadness.

Melonie may consider explaining what she is going through with her friends and asking for their support.

That way they may understand that she is not intending to withdraw from them.

Sometimes being excluded is because of your behaviour or attitude – and a signal that you may need to start making changes.

Melonie would benefit from setting goals for herself. Initially these could be quite small and achievable. Goals relating to exercise, good-quality sleep and nutrition would all be very worthwhile to consider.

Some longer-term goals she may consider might be to take up a new hobby or join a new sports team.

Key points to remember

Approach your friends to let them know how you feel.

Reflect on your behaviour and change it if it will help.

Set short-term and longer-term goals for yourself.

#8

Karrie - who experiences cyberbullying after posting a photo

Type: Cyber

As soon as I walked into class the following morning I sensed something was wrong.

I was new. Jimmy was hot. All the girls were chasing him. It began when Jimmy sidled up to me one lunchtime and told me that if I sent a personal photo of me he'd be my boyfriend. The way he paused on the word 'personal' made me feel hot and cold at the same time. Jimmy was so popular. It would be the most perfect way for me to get settled into high school. I knew that Jimmy would also get the message nice and clear that I liked him too if I sent him a photo of myself - just for him.

As I stood in front of the mirror staring at myself, a wave of fear washed over me. Was I doing something really dumb? But Jimmy seemed so nice and sincere. Maybe this was his way of making sure I was the right person for him. And of course the pic would be just between the two of us and would surely bring us closer. I took a topless picture of myself and sent it to Jimmy, hoping that he'd like the picture and would ask me to go out with him the following day.

As soon as I walked into class the following morning I sensed something was wrong. Whispers and giggles quickly subsided as I headed over to my table by the window. I felt everyone was looking at me. During the lesson I looked over to Jimmy at least 10 times but not once did he look my way.

'What's going on?' I eventually asked Vanessa, sitting next to me. 'What have you done?' she hissed.

'What are you talking about?' But I knew already. I turned to look at Jimmy again as Vanessa replied.

'My brother has a half-naked photo of you on his phone,' she replied, looking disgusted.

I was devastated. I rushed out of the room, not even caring what the teacher was saying to me as I slammed the door. I couldn't believe Jimmy had done that – I was so sure that I could trust him and now my best friend's brother had the picture and who else? Probably half of the school! What had I done?

I remembered the speaker who had visited school and spoke about online dangers, about sexting, and wished I had listened more. I didn't think that taking a private pic of myself was actually sexting – I'd heard that's what some kids did when they wanted to get into a relationship. I did remember the speaker saying that once pics like this go viral, it is almost impossible to control where they end up. And that if the pics were of an underage person that it was a criminal offence. Why hadn't I stopped to think first!

Vanessa was hardly going to be sympathetic. I'd been warned! I thought of all the people who may be on Jimmy's distribution list – potentially hundreds of people! The selfie is probably going around now – everyone will know. How can I face anyone again?

I walked into town thinking about the whole stupid situation. Why had I trusted Jimmy? How did I not think what might happen? One thing was for sure – Jimmy was not as great as I'd first thought. Had he intended to do this all along? Didn't he think that he might get caught? I stopped. Of course he thought he could get away with it. Who would grass on him? His friends with the pic wouldn't. Perhaps I was the best person to follow this up.

I sent a text to Jimmy telling him that I knew what he had done – and sarcastically thanked him for his respect towards me. I also thought I would bluff Jimmy by adding that unfortunately I was going to have to report what he had done to the school as transmitting pictures of this nature was an offence.

I guess I wasn't really going to do that, but thought that this was the best way to get Jimmy to tell his friends to delete the pics before they were sent on to other people. It was worth a try anyway. I was desperate.

That night Vanessa sent me a text. 'Don't know what you did, but my brother has deleted all his sus photos – well done, Karrie.'

. . . .

Sending naked selfies is never a good idea, as indicated above. Karrie may never know where they end up and who might see them. What if her parents look at her phone? What if she breaks up with her boyfriend? He may use them to get back at her. Furthermore, if the person taking the selfies was underage, there may be serious consequences for the people who receive them and pass them on to others.

If you do find out that your selfie has been posted or sent to other people – act fast! Contact the website operator and ask them to remove it. Or, as Karrie did, threaten to report the image and perhaps that might frighten people enough for them to remove it. More importantly, underage naked selfies have a huge legal consequence and it is important that you are fully informed.

Key points to remember

In this scenario it's up to you to take control.

Be aware of the legal aspects and consequences of sending underage naked selfies and ensure that all your friends know about them too.

If it happens, ensure that the images are deleted as soon as possible.

Don't do it!

#9

Ashli – who is verbally put down and humiliated

Type: Overt – Verbal

Anyway, I shrugged it off. I just told my mates that I didn't care.

ROBERT

Okay, I won't beat around the bush. I was interested in the new girl at school, Ashli. She and her friends often hung out with me and my friends and over time I found ways to catch Ashli's attention. I'd try to walk with her to class or sit with her if I could. She just needed to know that I was interested. But the right moment just never seemed to come up.

So on Friday I walked up to her directly and told her that I thought she was really nice and asked her if she wanted to come to my house on the weekend. She replied that she was busy and didn't want to hang out with me. I have to admit I felt hurt and embarrassed. What was worse was that two of my best friends called me a loser.

Anyway, I shrugged it off. I just told my mates that I didn't care. I told them it was lucky that she said no as now I could see the real side to her. I told them I was glad that she said no.

If I did see her after that, I basically told her she wasn't fitting in at her new school and needed to improve her attitude. It was for her own good.

ASHLI

I'm not sure exactly why he was targeting me, but Robert seemed to have it in for me from day one. He went from being friendly and cheerful to spooky - and then back to cheerful again. He was just one of the kids in a big group that I was mixing with. But when he asked me over to his place I suddenly realised he wanted something a whole lot more. I told him that I was busy and that anyway I wasn't interested. I was kind of firm but I hope I wasn't unkind.

After that it just got worse. He couldn't seem to handle the rejection. I would have been happy just being friends with him, as I was with the others. I wasn't ready for being with just one person. I needed the support of the whole group. But he just wouldn't let go. He told me that I'd made a big mistake, that I was obviously struggling to fit in, weird things like that. He would laugh at me, disagree with things I said. Whenever he could, he tried to put me down, especially if we were all together.

So I tried to avoid him, but of course that meant missing out on being with some of my other friends. I even changed one of my classes. But it didn't really change anything. I spoke to my friends about what had been happening and they weren't sure what to do either.

. . . .

At lunchtime later that week Ashli's friends noticed that she had not been around a lot lately. They had seen her in class, but she was often missing at lunchtime. One of her friends, Sarah, had seen her in the library, but only the one time.

Her friends started to worry about her and talked about how they could help and what they could do.

Sarah talked to her mum, who explained that Robert's behaviour was a form of bullying. The negative comments were really a show of power and control, especially as he had been 'rejected' by Ashli. She further explained that the girls were actually 'bystanders'; they knew about the bullying that was happening to Ashli. She added that as bystanders they were actually condoning the bullying and may have even played a part in encouraging Robert's nasty attacks. They had an important part to play in addressing the problem. Sarah was horrified that they could have played a role.

Ashli's friends wanted to know what they could do to help. Together they came up with a plan.

The first step was for someone to let Robert know that what he was doing was bullying and that Ashli was upset and isolating herself as a result of his behaviour. They thought that Robert also needed to know more about the effects of his bullying.

Secondly, they were going to let Robert know that they did not approve of what he was doing and that he should stop. They decided that as a school they needed to know more about bullying so, with the support of one of their teachers, they explored various anti-bullying activities and projects they could undertake in the classroom. Finally, they decided that they would tell Ashli what they had learned about bullying and that from now on she had their full support.

SUPPORTIVE BYSTANDERS

Just as we have human rights, we also have responsibilities to respect and protect the rights of others. An 'instepper' will take action to protect the rights of others.

Key points to remember

Make it clear to your friends that you won't be involved in bullying behaviour.

Never stand by and watch or encourage bullying behaviour.

Do not harass, tease or spread gossip about others - this includes on social networking sites like Facebook.

Never forward or respond to messages or photos that may be offensive or upsetting - always delete them.

Encourage the person who is being bullied to ask for help, for example go with them to a place they can get help or provide them with information about where to go for help.

Report bullying to someone in authority or someone you trust, for example at school to a teacher or a school counsellor, at work to a manager. If the bullying is serious, report it to the police. If the bullying occurs on social media, report it to the site mediator.

#10

Leila – who is bullied with hurtful lies

Type: Overt - Written

'We don't want sluts here — go home, Leila.'

LEILA JOHNSTON

Age	15
Star Sign	Leo
Likes	Fashion, Sport, Modelling, Keeping Fit

JENNY LEEFOOT

Age	16
Star Sign	Capricorn
Likes	Football, Boys, Parties

'Leila just annoys me. The way she follows us around, the way she dresses. She thinks she's so goddamn beautiful.'

'Jenny, that's because she actually is.'

'Is what?'

'Beautiful.'

'Shut up, Dee. Do you want to know the truth about Leila?' Dee and the others leaned forward, eager for some gossip. If anyone knew what was going on, Jenny did. 'She's actually a bit of a slut. She's had four boyfriends already this year. All of them in the football team.'

Leila couldn't believe it when she heard what Jenny had been saying about her behind her back. She was even more shocked when she read what had been scrawled in thick black text across the inside cover of her English book.

'Go and find another school, whore.'

She suspected that Jenny was behind it but had no way of proving it. A few days later she was horrified to see a notice pinned up on the wall outside the canteen.

'We don't want sluts here - go home, Leila.'

Leila's friend Jane caught up with her during lunch. 'What are you going to do about it? It must be awful for you.'

Leila agreed that she was really embarrassed about what was being said about her, but she also felt angry that the people writing these things didn't have the courage to say it to her face. Leila thought about her options. She wasn't prepared to put up with what was going on, but she didn't want to add to the problem by confronting Jenny and making a scene. She knew that would just add more fuel to the situation and it would all get out of proportion. She needed a way to let Jenny know that she suspected she was behind the gossiping, but also not inflame the situation.

That weekend Leila let her older sister in on what had been going on at school. 'I know Jenny is behind it, but I just don't trust her if I confront her with what I know. She will make my life hell.' Leila's sister suggested she try 'fogging'. She explained that fogging discourages the person without antagonising them.

'What you do is make a joke or a funny comment that makes the other person think you don't care about what is being said. Or you pretend to agree with them so they have nothing to bother you about.'

'How would it work?' asked Leila.

'Well, next time you see a notice up in the canteen you could say loudly and near Jenny something like, "Oh no...my secret is out!" Or, "Gee, they have found out what I am really like." Then just walk away laughing.'

'Oh, I see,' said Leila, 'I just pretend to go along with it and when they see that I am not worried and even find it all a bit funny, they will stop.'

Leila's sister explained that Jenny's comments and gossiping is just her way of making herself more important and appearing like she has more power. By making it all a joke the power is taken away from her.

In English class the next day, Leila opened her text to where the comment about her being a whore was written. She leaned over to Jane, making sure that Jenny could hear, and said, 'Hey, Jane, look what is written in my book...they can't even spell whore!' and started laughing. She then said loudly, 'Well, if I am a whore, I'd better get to work. Jane, where is the party this weekend?'

For the next day or so, Leila made jokes about what she heard or read. It wasn't easy as deep inside she was hurt; however, she knew that the girls involved were just trying to upset her and Leila was determined that she wasn't going to let that show.

Leila was surprised how quickly the fogging worked. She also found it fun making jokes out of what was being said; however, she was very happy when it ended.

Leila also thought it funny when one of Jenny's friends suggested she come over to her place on the weekend for a gathering...

Key points to remember

Making a joke out of a situation can help diffuse the situation - this technique is known as fogging.

Be aware of your emotions but don't let your negative emotions stop you from acting in a situation.

#11

Billy - who experiences racial vilification

Type: Overt - Verbal

I laughed with them, but it hurt and it was clear I was not one of them.

Hi, my name is Billy. I am a Torres Strait Islander now living and attending school in Melbourne. There are a lot of kids from different backgrounds at my school, but none from Torres Strait. I really miss going home and hunting with my mates; the water is so blue and clear and we can eat turtles. I know it is good for me to be here and get a good education, but I miss my grandmother and she cried when she found out I was moving to Melbourne.

Everyone is okay to me. Yeah, kind of. They asked me what it feels like to be wearing clothes, as if we don't wear clothes at home. They also joke about pretending to be a kangaroo and calling out 'Catch me if you can!' They don't even know we don't have kangaroos on our island. It makes me laugh cos they are so dumb.

I had to stay back for detention last week cos I wouldn't shave my beard. I tried to tell the teachers that in our culture my mother's brother has to shave me for the first time. This is so important and has been a part of our culture for thousands of years. It is recognition that I am an adult. I am going home next month for the ceremony. There will be singing and a feast prepared for all the boys who will be having their first shave. I found some information for the teachers and they now understand, but they still tell me to go and have a shave and that I look a mess. Maybe it's a bit of a joke for them.

This reminds me of a day when I was invited to a mate's house after school. It was night time and they turned off the lights and then laughingly said, 'Hey, Billy, open your eyes so we can see where you are!' I laughed with them, but it hurt and it was clear I was not one of them. But you know what? Actually I am really happy that I'm not. They've never been outside of Melbourne and have no idea what it's like where I am from. It's beautiful and our culture is old and interesting. I will be going back in a year or so and bring with me a good education which I can use to help people. Being teased about my culture and skin colour is no fun. It just reflects on their lack of education and biased outlook. I'm lucky really that I can stand back and see it.

. . . .

Billy has realised that bullies can be foolish and has chosen to feel sorry for them instead of feeling belittled by them. Research shows that bullies tend to have poorer academic skills and have problems with the way they think. They lack empathy. Bullies are also at a heightened risk for substance use and criminal behaviour as they get older. Another interesting fact about bullies is that as they get older they become more and more unpopular.

The boys bullying Billy are really demonstrating a lack of recognition of cultural awareness, which reflects on their attitudes and biases. Billy has done well to see this for what it is and has chosen not to take their joking on board. There is a great saying which is, 'Life will throw balls at you, but you don't have to catch them.' This is just what Billy has done.

Key points to remember

Teasing about a person's culture, background, ethnicity and race is still bullying.

If low level, sometimes we just need to feel sorry for the bullies, they don't always know any better.

Bullies come with their own set of problems they have to cope with.

#12

Anton – who has a hate page written about him

Type: Cyber

One day he thought he would search his own name and see what might come up.

Anton never felt that he 'belonged' anywhere; his parents were from Russia and didn't speak English. Although Anton had been at the same school since kindergarten, he couldn't invite anyone home as they would not be able to understand his parents and they would not like the food his mother cooked. Who would like cabbage and fish soup? Anton had a couple of friends who he sat with at lunchtime, but their discussion was nothing more than 'Did you finish your English homework?' Anton didn't really have the confidence to make more friends as he felt that the other students didn't want to be around him. He felt like he didn't have very much to offer.

Anton started to spend a lot of time at home surfing the net and playing games. He also started to look forward to Year 7 when he would get the chance to make new friends. He dreamed of how he might meet a friend who he could do things together with. Maybe they'd even like cabbage and fish soup.

Year 7 came and went and Anton still felt alone and didn't find his special friend. He spent even more time shut away in his bedroom on his computer. One day he thought he would search his own name and see what might come up. He was devastated. He uncovered an 'Anton Smells of Cabbage Hate Page'. The site was full of jokes and comments about himself and his family. Anton couldn't believe that people thought of him this way. No one had ever said anything. The comments were hateful and he felt even more awful.

Anton hated coming from Russia and just wished he lived a normal life with a normal family. He hated his school and more than anything hated himself.

. . . .

Not that any type of bullying is better than any other, but this type of bullying can leave long-lasting, psychological damage.

Hate pages of this nature can be accessed by any number of people and can elicit comments and criticisms from people who don't even know you. They just want to vent for the sake of it. Racism is one such issue that can be easily expressed anonymously, with the instigator's identity screened from everyone. It needs to be clearly and repeatedly explained that this type of bullying is not personal; it's racial. However, when it's happening to you the distinction will make little difference to how you feel about it.

As well as being racially targeted by people at school, it is possible that Anton is a victim of trolling. An Internet troll is a person who posts comments either using a pseudonym or anonymously with the aim of using shock value to promote bigotry, racism and general hatred. They love to create dramas in any public environment and a 'hate' is a perfect medium. Trolls are just about impossible to educate regarding the damage they are doing. The best way to stop trolls and racist bullies is to report the site to the mediators of the system. They have ways to block the sites and stop the remarks being seen.

Anton mentions that he has started to spend a lot of time on his own at home, and that at school he feels he doesn't have a lot to offer in regards to friendships. This may also indicate that he is depressed. Depression can be a typical outcome to an untypical situation. In general, depression affects how people feel about themselves. People can lose interest in things they used to enjoy doing. They can lack energy, feel sad and avoid social situations. People might even think that they are a failure, that they're worthless or that life is not worth living.

Sometimes you have to teach yourself how to feel good about yourself.

Here are some tips:

* **Keep going:** Don't let life's challenges throw you off track.

* **Trust yourself:** Believe in your inner resources, no matter what, and you'll grow from the experience.

* **Watch your thoughts:** Learn to dismiss the negative thoughts and stay open to other ideas that will help you move in a positive direction.

* **Summon the strength you have inside:** Believe that your strength and intelligence can help you deal with anything.

* **Recognise that disappointment is part of life:** Even the most successful people have to deal with disappointment; the trick is to learn how to use it to stay on track.

★ **Deal with your fears**: Overcoming fear makes you stronger, and being a little scared can make you better. You want to have butterflies; you just don't want them flying in formation. It helps to understand and admit your fears. Then you can kick them to the kerb.

Finally, Anton should let his parents know what is going on. Unfortunately they may also have experienced some form of racism and will understand what it is like for him. They may also have some strategies that have worked for them that he can try out. It might also be beneficial to discuss moving to a new school, where Anton could leave the past behind and start a new future.

Key points to remember

Educate yourself about trolls and trolling.

It's okay to report them to a site administrator.

Acknowledge that you might be feeling bad about what's happening and perhaps take a first step of exploring a website such as beyondblue (see page 153).

Don't forget that your parents can be a great help also.

#13

Matt – who is excluded from his online game

Type: Cyber

So I messaged Greg and told him that I wouldn't be able to start our assault on Level 12 till the following week.

Level 11! Not bad for someone who'd only been playing the Internet game 'War of All Worlds' for six months. It was the best. Not only did you get to meet people from all over the world but also I was gaining heaps of credit for my skills. Gaining credit meant gaining power and that was what being good at War of All Worlds was all about. When I logged on I had respect from everyone. For the first 11 levels, you could fight solo, but from Level 12 onwards, you needed to find a partner.

A guy called Greg asked me if we could join up. He said we'd be unbeatable as a team. I figured he was right. We would be a dominant force, indestructible. We were ready to take on Level 12. It didn't matter that Greg was some kid from the other side of the world. The only downside was that I had to wait up till 1 am in the morning before we could join up and take on everyone else. That was okay. I'm not a kid who needs much sleep anyway. The only other issue was that first semester exams were about to start.

So I messaged Greg and told him that I wouldn't be able to start our assault on Level 12 till the following week. What difference was a few days going to make anyway? I told him we could just work on our skills in other levels until then. But Greg was furious. He told me I had totally let him down. That I had broken a promise.

The following night I saw that Greg had posted messages looking for someone who was willing to be 'available when required'. He was obviously over teaming up with losers like me. I also noticed that he had inboxed me saying that I was lucky that I lived on the other side of the planet and that it was the only place I could be safe.

So I messaged and explained again that I would be good to go just as soon as my exams were done. He didn't reply. For a couple of days I didn't log on, but when I got back into the game on Friday night, I noticed that Greg had a new partner. What made it worse was that there were notes about me being unreliable, a guy who couldn't stick it out through the tough times, a loser. Even Greg's new gaming partner, a guy I had never even messaged, agreed that I was '5 mins ago...and a gaming nobody.' I felt bad. I was so powerful in the game and now felt like I had nowhere I belonged.

. . . .

It appears that the choice to stop gaming or at least playing War of All Worlds has been made for Matt, and he now has more time to study for his exams, which is really a great outcome. Matt's feelings that he doesn't belong are common in people who spend a lot of time gaming. Internet games that have virtual worlds and associated online communities can simulate a feeling of acceptance, mateship, prestige and power. Outside of those worlds people can be disconnected from their community, unable to wield such power and might, highlighting feelings of detachment from the real world. Time away from gaming should eventually change these current feelings.

The other issue here is that Matt was being cyberbullied and it needed to stop. There is a particular name for cyberbullies who target gamers. They are known as 'griefers'. Griefers really use the game as a vehicle to cyberbully; they make the gaming experience awful for the other person. It sounds like Greg may have been a griefer.

In this case, all the difficult decisions have been made for Matt. Greg has a new gaming partner and Matt will now have the time he needs to undertake his studies. The distraction that his study will provide will also give him the emotional distance from gaming which will be beneficial to his mental health in general.

Key points to remember

Tell someone what is going on.

Never respond to their messages and attacks.

Block them.

Report them to the site's moderator.

#14

Rachael – who has her photo taken and posted

Type: Cyber

'Hey, everyone has different body shapes.' I tried not to get angry.

WEDNESDAY 3 MARCH

Three layers even though it was so hot, but how else do I cover up this disgusting body? Two days to go till Sports Day. I'll get the usual comments; I guess they mean well. How I'm way too conscious of my body. Yeah, easy for them to say; they don't have to live inside it like I do. So what will it be? Dentist? No, did that last week. Sick? A bit lame. Mum will be okay. She always writes a note for me. Whatever.

THURSDAY 4 MARCH

Cooler today, but spent most of the day in the library. Gab comes up and says, 'Hey, Rach, just chill out and have fun.' And I'm like, 'Thanks, Gab.' But she keeps on hammering away like she wants to solve all the problems of the world. 'Hey, everyone has different body shapes.' I tried not to get angry. I just muttered something and went back to my assignment.

FRIDAY 5 MARCH

Worst bloody day of my life. I left my note at home! I tried to explain to Ms Fenwick that I haven't been well. I told her to ring my mum even, but she didn't listen. I realised that I was going to have to get into my sports gear in the changing rooms. I was panicking. God. This was so stupid. I left the changing to the last minute. I could wear my big sports jacket over the top and I'd just go tell Miss Cramer that I wasn't well and I'd help her out instead. She was nice and would understand.

So I'm getting dressed in a corner of the changing room and there's this flash. I look round, real scared. Geez, is someone taking a bloody photo of me? 'Hello?' I call out, kind of soft. No one answers and I don't see anyone about. Maybe I'm going crazy, I think, shoving my clothes into my bag. I get out of there real quick.

First person I see is Amanda, smiling at me. 'Hey, you made it! We thought you weren't going to show up.' She and a few others were laughing as they turned away towards the ovals.

I head over to my house group and there are the girls again, giggling and grinning and looking at their phones. As I approach them they quickly turn away. All day I sense there is something going on, but I don't know exactly what. I stay pretty close to Miss Cramer and help her out. As soon as I can, I get the hell out of there. I even walked home.

So that night, for the 200th time, I decide to go on a diet. A proper, sensible one this time. All those kids running and jumping today, they looked like they were actually having fun. Maybe I'd enjoy it too if I had a better body shape.

Before I log on I check my email. I'm surprised to see one from Gab. 'Hi Rach, I am really sorry to let you know this, but while you were changing today, Amanda took a picture of you and sent it around to all of us... I know this is wrong and

I deleted my pic...but some of the others have sent it to their boyfriends... They think it's funny... I am so sorry to tell you this... Please don't let Amanda know I have contacted you... I really think you need to do something about this... Perhaps tell Ms Fenwick? PLEASE don't tell anyone I told you.'

SATURDAY 6 MARCH

I think I must have cried for about two hours last night. Finally got to sleep. I woke up this morning and had the most amazing thought that it had all been this horrible dream. Then I saw myself in the mirror. Mum took one look at me and dragged me off to the living room.

'Rachael?' she said, all concerned. I told her everything.

. . . .

Rachael has taken the first and biggest step in letting someone know what is happening. She will certainly benefit from having support in working through some of these issues and she WILL get through them. Thank goodness Gab sent that email. Perhaps this might be the start of her making some of the changes that she has been considering.

Research indicates that people who are overweight or underweight tend to be at higher risk for bullying; this type of bullying is sometimes referred to as 'weight teasing'.

Weight teasing can change how you feel about your body and the way you look. People who have been 'weight teased' over time may also be at a higher risk for developing unhealthy eating and exercise habits. This can also lead to disorders such as anorexia, bulimia and binge eating. Furthermore, weight teasing can lead to a lowered self-esteem, depression and self-harming behaviours, which can be typical responses. This type of bullying can also lead to a vicious circle or pattern of behaviour where a person who feels bad about themselves starts to comfort eat, which in turn heightens the feelings of guilt and shame.

In this case we need to address the bullying situation first. It is too hard to address Rachael's body image concerns while she is still being teased. Now that her mum knows the whole story, perhaps Rachael can go to the school and meet with her teacher, school counsellor or welfare teacher to explore appropriate strategies.

One strategy might be for the school to give a general talk at assembly on bullying and its effects; another might be for the counsellor to have a quiet talk to the girls involved; or sometimes just having posters around the school can send a strong reminder that bullying is not tolerated. Rachael will need to let her mum know if she wishes to be identified or not. The strategies taken must be ones that she is happy with. This is the time for Rachael to take back control.

Once the bullying has been dealt with, Rachael can then start thinking about making healthy choices regarding her diet and exercise (see pages 121-9 for tips). Perhaps in the short term she could seek out the support of a dietician or personal trainer. These qualified professionals can teach Rachael the best ways to make healthy choices and keep her on track. It's good to develop an initial eight-week plan to establish new behavioural habits.

There are also some great websites worth looking at, such as:

* **www.eatforhealth.gov.au/guidelines/australian-guide-healthy-eating:** This site details the Australian dietary guidelines and offers advice about the amount and kinds of foods that we need to eat for health and wellbeing. It also has calculators to help you estimate your energy (kilojoule) needs, nutrient requirements and the number of servings from the Five Food Groups you need daily.

★ **www.healthyfoodguide.com.au/resources/exercise-planner:** This site has a three-month exercise and diet plan as well as lots of inspiration.

It would also be beneficial for Rachael to continue meeting with her school counsellor or perhaps ask for a referral for counselling from her doctor. Counselling will really help with strategies to boost self-esteem and deal with the emotional issues related to being bullied, along with giving her another person on her 'support team'.

Perhaps she could even start setting some goals so that she can see her development and celebrate her achievements.

Key points to remember

It's always good to talk through problems with a trusted adult.

The first step to changing a situation is often the hardest.

Enlist a favourite teacher or your school counsellor to address the bullying problem.

Remember you can take back control as well as solving the problem.

#15

Orval - who receives threatening messages

Type: Cyber

The next day I got a reply, but this time it was personal.

Why do I like Tumblr so much? I guess it's because it gives me a chance to post images and sayings about things that matter to me. It gives me a chance to express my feelings and what I'm thinking about at any particular time of the day or night. I guess l look at the world a bit differently to most people. I don't think people in general realise how hard, tough and actually sad life can be. When I spend time browsing through other people's images along a similar theme, I actually feel better myself.

For a week or so I was getting some positive comments from people so I worked even harder to develop my site. I called it 'The Light from the Dark Side'. But then I read a comment which shocked me.

'Your site is lame and you shouldn't be promoting such crap.' I replied straightaway, telling this person that my site was actually helping a lot of people work through their dark times. The next day I got a reply, but this time it was personal.

'Hey, Emo Loser, if you feel so bad why don't you just curl up in a ball and die in a gutter somewhere where no one will find you.'

After that I didn't respond to any more messages. The last one really upset me. After all, I was only trying to help people. Obviously this person was in need of some help but just not willing to take it on board at the moment. Even though I knew that the site had helped others, it was not a great place for me to be anymore.

. . . .

It's wonderful that Orval has created a site that he knows has helped young people deal with situations life can throw at them. It's just a shame that his great work has been trashed by people who don't understand what he is trying to achieve. Not everyone is going to agree with him, but if it is important to Orval and he knows that what he is doing is beneficial to others, he needs to keep going.

Negative comments can make us feel inferior, silly and humiliated. What we are doing when we feel this way is agreeing with the bully. After all they must be right... Not!

Here are some recommendations for Orval:

* **Assess the situation:** Who is this person/people? Perhaps they're 'trolls', people whose intention is to upset other people by posting inflammatory remarks.

* **Stop wishing they would understand:** There are some people's opinions and views and attitudes you'll never change and in trying you may lose sight of your own goals.

* **Distance yourself from their comments:** By trying to be emotionally detached you give yourself some space and perhaps a different perspective.

* **Keep your cool:** Don't defend yourself or retaliate – it will only make them respond more aggressively. They may just enjoy the game of upsetting you and what you are trying to achieve.

* **Keep it in perspective:** Evaluate the comments of one or two people against all the people in the future who might benefit from what you are offering.

In order to keep moving forward you may need to change how you feel about the comments (see page 135 regarding your self-talk). It's also helpful if you view the bullies as people who don't know any better and perhaps need support themselves. In reframing your experiences, you will be able to continue with your work as well as learning more about yourself. Don't give up; they're not worth it.

It's also important to know that the Australian Government has established the Children's eSafety Commissioner, whose role it is to conduct investigations into cyberbullying. The government office can request that the offensive material be removed from social media. If this is not done, civil penalties may apply. You can contact the Office of the Children's eSafety Commissioner by email: *enquiries@esafety.gov.au*, or telephone: *1800 880 176*.

Key points to remember

Always assess the situation before taking action.

Keep your cool.

Try to reframe your experience; there are always going to be people who put you down in some way.

If it escalates, remember that we have a government body that can assist with cyberbullying issues.

#16

Lauryn – who is excluded by her friends

Type: Covert

The following Monday I told the girls that I was good to go with my new phone and that they could start messaging me.

It was Casual Clothes Day and I always got a bit anxious on these days. I try to look my best and wear what I think looks right and okay.

When I got to school I kept an eye out on the cool group of girls to see what they were wearing. I figured that I didn't look so out of place. My jeans were okay, but they all seemed to be kind of matching with what they were wearing. Later that day I found out that they'd all texted each other and organised their outfits the night before. I figured that if I was able to text as well I'd be a part of the main group. So that night I begged Mum to let me get a phone so I could text and she promised that at the end of the month I could have one. I'd be able to hook up with the girls anytime, go to films with them and basically properly fit in with them, rather than be a bit on the outside, which is how I felt things were at the moment. It was hard but exciting counting down the days. I was sure that once I got my new phone I'd be right in straight away with the popular girls. They all had smart phones; it was the only thing different about me and them.

Finally the day arrived for Mum and me to pick out my phone. The guy explained the plan and I promised Mum that I'd keep an eye on my account. She said she'd be keeping an eye on it too!

The following Monday I told the girls that I was good to go with my new phone and that they could start messaging me. I gave them all the details via the school email.

No messages came through for me that first night, which surprised me a little bit. I figured maybe the girls were doing homework or something. Tomorrow would be different.

Tuesday came and went and there were still no messages. Maybe I'd got the details of my account wrong, but I knew I hadn't. So I emailed my details through again. The following morning there was a message for me.

'Hey, Lauryn, we don't think you, well...like...you don't really fit with us.' And another with a name I didn't even know, 'Forget it, Lauryn, we don't have time for you.'

I stared at the phone feeling confused and a bit humiliated. Is this what they thought of me?

. . . .

It's important for Lauryn to feel that she fits in with a group and doesn't feel like an outsider, but the first step is for her to evaluate herself.

Is she a person that:

* Has a passionate interest, or a creative way of seeing things that certain people would judge 'different' or 'unusual' since it falls outside of the narrow range of what they know?

* Is able to connect with people that others don't seem to understand or appreciate?

* Is more open than most people to exploring new ideas or trying out solutions that others are afraid of or consider too risky?

* Is reluctant to partake in the pettiness, competitiveness, or mean-spirited comments that others engage in and which would keep her from fitting in?

* Can look around and wonder how certain people know so easily how to be accepted, almost as if they got the instruction book that you never received?

If Lauryn answered 'yes' to any of the questions, she should feel proud of her individuality! Her uniqueness may actually be a strength that will guide her on a different (and perhaps more rewarding) pathway.

It is not uncommon to have the feeling 'I don't belong here', and the feeling is likely to be a trigger for us to evaluate what we are trying to achieve and to make some changes.

We need to be aware of what our intention or goals are. Why is it important that I belong to a particular group? What can I offer them? Do they have similar values and ethics as me? Do I want to be associated with them? Are they good people? It appears in this situation that the group is just not right for Lauryn. Does she really want to be associated with such girls?

After evaluating herself and what she stands for, the next step is to identify people who hold some of the same values and interests that Lauryn has and make a move to include them in her life in some way.

Remember, it's okay to be messy, out there, cool, loud, clumsy, fun, crazy, whatever you want to be – just be yourself.

Key points to remember

Not everyone is nice.

Get to know yourself and what you stand for.

Remember you are unique and you can strive to be the best you.

#17

Tyrone - who receives unwelcome text messages

Type: Cyber

'What other secrets do you have?'

Tyrone really liked one of the girls in his class, Natalie. He often waited outside the canteen in the hope that she might pass by. He also sat with her in English and offered to help her with her homework. Tyrone hadn't told his friends about his feelings for Natalie; he wanted to keep it to himself. More and more, Tyrone avoided spending time with his friends at lunchtime while he looked for Natalie in the hope she might have lunch with him.

Tyrone's friends started to ask questions about where he was. Tyrone told them he was catching up with some work he hadn't finished or some other excuse. The following week Tyrone was delighted when Natalie asked him if he could help her with her English essay. They decided to go to the library to work together during lunchtime. They both agreed that the time had gone by so quickly and that they'd meet again in the same spot the following day.

But Tyrone's friends were keen to find out what he was up to. The next day they decided to go searching for him. After 10 minutes of looking, they discovered them both at a table in the non-fiction section of the library. It was all they needed to see. They knew something was going on.

Tyrone's friends started sending him text messages. 'We know where you are.' 'Having fun, Tyrone?' 'Who's the dark horse?' 'What other secrets do you have?'

The messages didn't stop. Before school, during school, after school and into the evening. 'Where are you now, you Playboy?'

'Hey, T, you busy...?' 'What about spending some time with your real friends?' Tyrone knew they'd respond in this way once they realised he was spending more and more time with Natalie. Maybe he should have been even more careful.

Tyrone was really happy with how things were developing with Natalie and didn't want his mates to spoil anything. He was also getting really annoyed with the constant barrage of stupid text messages. He thought it was daft to think that his friendships with his mates should be ruined just because he was seeing more of Natalie.

. . . .

There is a fine line between annoying text messages and bullying, and it is often how you feel about what is happening that decides what is going on. In this case, Tyrone appears to be annoyed, but he does not express any concerns regarding his self-esteem, humiliation or feeling put down. Furthermore, he is not letting the boys' teasing get in the way of his intentions to get to know Natalie better.

When Tyrone thinks through the situation more, he will realise that he doesn't want to lose his friends; however, he also wants to see Natalie more often. He knows the boys don't mean to upset him. On the other hand, the texts are becoming more frequent and that will most likely be very annoying. He knows he really needs space from the boys' teasing or it will get a whole lot worse.

Here's an approach that describes what Tyrone did and the outcome that resulted from the stance he took.

Tyrone decided to agree with what the boys were saying; that way he wasn't arguing with them or defending himself, which may have made the situation escalate. By agreeing with what they were saying, Tyrone used a technique called 'fogging'. Fogging is when you give someone an agreeable response when they are being aggressive. For example, when the boys sent the message, 'Where are you now, you Playboy?' he responded, 'I'm where all the best playboys hang out. See you at footy training tomorrow.' This unexpected response was intended to surprise the boys as well as sidestep the issue. Tyrone also highlighted that he valued their friendship by mentioning that he will see them tomorrow. Tyrone's response was also assertive; he was firm, open and used humour to lighten up the situation.

In another response, Tyrone let the boys know that he was 'busy and just about to turn off his phone.' Again he didn't defend himself; however, he was clear and firm with his response. It didn't take long for the boys to realise that Tyrone was not to be messed with and that their intention to annoy had no effect. They got on with their lives and let Tyrone enjoy getting to know Natalie more.

Key points to remember

One possible outcome of teasing is that it can encourage us to think about our own behaviour and therefore make appropriate changes. Sometimes friends don't realise how their comments can hurt us - it's okay to let them know.

Try 'fogging' or agreeing with what the 'bullies' are saying.

#18

Wen – who receives threatening emails

Type: Overt – Written

I felt bad but I did inbox her back saying that she was a princess and needed to get a life.

I thought Lucie and I would always be best friends. Wen the Hen and Luce the Goose. We'd known each other for ages; our families even holidayed together. But it all began to unravel a few weeks ago when Lucie got her boyfriend Mike. Of course she was going to spend more time with him and therefore less time with me. I started to feel a bit left out. Occasionally we'd do things together. Maybe go to the movies or head into town together after school on Friday. I thought I would be a bit of a third wheel, but it was better than staying home on my own.

But I was surprised how well Mike and I got on. He had a great sense of humour and soon we became good friends on Facebook. Lucie quickly became really jealous and began inboxing me telling me to leave Mike alone. She thought I was trying to break them up. This wasn't true; I just thought Mike was a great guy.

I felt bad but I did inbox her back saying that she was a princess and needed to get a life. Of course, this only made everything worse. Lucie got really angry and said that she would tell Mike I was the biggest bitch out. She was acting like such a loser but I kept in touch with Mike, thinking that she'd get over it soon enough. It wasn't as if I was chasing him or anything, even if that's what she thought. It was all so awful. Mum and Dad kept asking me when they'd be seeing Lucie again but I couldn't let them know that we weren't talking.

Then I got a message from her telling me that she was going to smash me in the face if I spoke to Mike again and told me I had better watch my back at school next week. I couldn't believe that she was so angry with me. Mike and I were only Facebook friends. The attacks from Lucie kept coming and each one was nastier. I sat down and thought carefully about how I'd reply, but I just didn't know where to start.

So I wrote back saying that this was it. The end. Goodbye forever. I feel bad that I have lost my best friend, but her arguing and attacks were getting worse. I thought it would be better for me to end everything before it all got too bad. Mum and Dad keep asking what has happened to Lucie, but I don't tell them about the Facebook stuff in case they take my laptop away from me. I just tell them that she is busy with Mike. I know I didn't do anything to take Mike away from her. I guess she's just insecure.

. . . .

Sometimes there are no strategies to resolve things. It's just messy and we have to get through it the best way we can. Wen has tried to explain to Lucie that her friendship with Mike is just that, a friendship; however, Lucie didn't want to listen. She is most likely feeling insecure.

Sometimes insecurity comes from other deep-rooted issues such as a person's home life, previous relationships and emotional problems. If you understand the cause, you may be able to empathise and help the situation. However, Lucie is not really providing any opportunity to understand the situation due to her constant attacks, a form of defence. Wen made an appropriate decision to distance herself from the relationship – she is making a positive choice for herself not to be attacked and bullied. At the moment her relationship with Lucie is not healthy and supportive and so it is reasonable that she asserts herself by getting out of the firing line.

A friend should lift your spirits, make you laugh, remind you that you are loved and make you feel comfortable with yourself. A good friend won't lie to you and also won't try and hurt your feelings. Of course, friendships come with a few bumps and bruises on occasions and don't forget that you also have to be the best friend you can be.

It's a false notion that a friend is a friend forever. If a relationship brings you more pain than pleasure, it's time to reconsider.

Key points to remember

Solutions to problems can be messy and a successful outcome is not guaranteed. However, if a situation needs to be changed, sometimes we have to take the first steps to change it.

Being assertive is a great response to a negative situation; it may hurt at the start, but in the long run be worthwhile.

Friends are there to support, care for and inspire us; anything less than this should be questioned.

#19

Neil – who is pushed around and taunted

Type: Overt – Physical/Verbal

'That's the way, Neil. You're all over this kid,' his father bellowed.

Arlie is mad about football. He loves watching it, listening to it and most of all playing it. The Bulldogs are his favourite team and he knows all there is to know about them. At his primary school every second kid barracked for the Bulldogs. The school was situated in the heart of Bulldog territory and only a kilometre from the Bulldogs' home ground.

Now that he was in secondary school, Arlie was aware that there wouldn't be as many Bulldog supporters as his new school was over 10 kilometres from where he grew up. But he didn't think that was any reason not to continue showing his support for his team. Any chance he got he'd wear his Bulldogs gear to school.

Arlie had brought his autographed Bulldogs top to school to wear later for the first training session of the season, but when he went to pull on his football gear after school he was shocked to see that his top was missing. He searched the room frantically but to no avail. He asked his team mates if they'd seen his top, but they just shrugged. Fighting back tears, Arlie arrived on the ground wearing his school shirt.

The warm-up and skills session went well for Arlie, though he couldn't take his mind off his missing guernsey. When the practice match started, Arlie managed to get a couple of early touches.

'Nice and clean, Arlie,' one of the coaches shouted, as he dished off a pass. 'Well done.' A split second later, Arlie was knocked to the ground.

'Call yourself a Bulldog? More like a little puppy, wimp,' scoffed a freckly faced kid. He had his knee on Arlie's chest. Arlie tried to get up but the boy shoved him back.

'Get off me!' Arlie shouted, struggling to get back to his feet. The boy jogged away. Arlie managed to keep clear of the boy for the rest of the session. Another boy found his Bulldogs jumper shoved down one of the toilets.

'Just because I barrack for the Bulldogs?' Arlie muttered to himself as he walked home.

That Saturday the school had organised an intra-school practice match and sure enough the blond-haired, freckly faced kid was on the opposing side to Arlie's. A few seconds after the game commenced, the freckly faced boy jogged over in Arlie's direction.

'I'll play on this side.' He grinned. 'You go take the other wing,' he said to Arlie's original opponent. The blond-haired boy started elbowing Arlie, even though the ball was at the other end of the ground.

'That's it, Neil. Keep him honest!' Arlie looked over to the sidelines. A tall man was slapping his fist into his hand, staring at Neil. His father, Arlie thought to himself.

The ball was now heading in their direction. Arlie struggled to break away from Neil, who was holding him back.

'You've got no idea,' Neil muttered, pushing Arlie aside suddenly and lurching for the ball. Arlie recovered his balance but was too late to stop Neil from kicking the ball back to the middle of the ground.

'That's the way, Neil. You're all over this kid,' his father bellowed. The next time the ball came in their direction, Arlie was ready. He feinted to go one way, and then spun round, leaving Neil alone and bewildered. Arlie took control of the ball, fired off a neat pass, then ran on towards the goal.

'Get up, you Princess!' he heard Neil's father roar at his son. 'That was pathetic!'

Arlie said nothing as he jogged further forward. He'd just helped his side score the first goal of the game.

It was going to be a tough game. Arlie decided to concentrate totally on the football. He'd think about what he'd do about Neil after the game.

. . . .

This is one bullying situation where understanding the causes of bullying behaviour can help the victim cope with the situation. This understanding will also help Arlie realise that to address the issue will take more than a short-term intervention. Neil's bullying of Arlie is a learned behaviour from his father and has become embedded as a result of a lifetime of parental modelling. In fact, Neil may not even know that his behaviour is bullying; it may be the only way he knows how to interact with people.

Parents who try to motivate their child by being sarcastic and disdainful can affect the child's self-esteem and self-belief. Furthermore, if a child learns how to treat people from the example of a bullying parent, they are likely to grow to be a bully as well, and may have a hard time developing healthy relationships.

So perhaps choosing to take a more passive approach and ignoring Neil's behaviour is the best strategy. It is hoped that

Neil will see that his taunts have no effect and his bullying behaviour should decrease.

What Arlie may not know is that when Neil gets older his bullying behaviour is more likely to result in:

* the abuse of alcohol and drugs

* getting into fights

* vandalising property

* dropping out of school

* having a criminal conviction

* being abusive to his own family.

The predicted long-term quality of life for a bully is not good.

In this scenario it would be beneficial for Arlie to focus on his game and even perhaps feel sadness for Neil and his aggressive father.

Key points to remember

Bullying is nearly always a learned behaviour – and often from the bully's parents!

Sometimes ignoring the bullying behaviour is the best strategy.

As bullies get older, their lives are often problematic.

#20

Mazie – who has a modified image of her posted online

Type: Cyber

As she read the first one, her
stomach turned to jelly.

Mazie enjoyed lots of things that she and her friends did together. She felt she was one of the 'in-crowd'. Often the girls would talk about how they'd do absolutely anything for anyone in their group, how they would stick together, no matter what. After all, isn't that what good friends were all about? Being there for you when you needed them most?

When they met they would often have long conversations about absolutely anything and everything. Mazie was on the quieter side so did a lot more listening than talking. It wasn't that she had nothing to say; it was more that her thoughts were often spoken by someone before she had a chance to express them herself.

Sometimes they looked at each other's Facebook pages. They could find out who had been with who at recent parties. There were always hundreds of recently added photos to check out. Like the others, Mazie loved looking at them - what people were wearing, who they were with and some of the weird and crazy poses the boys did to show off in front of the camera.

One evening one of the girls casually asked Mazie for her password. Mazie was reluctant as she'd heard that you should never share a password. But these girls were her best friends, out to protect her. What's more, the girls said that they all shared their passwords and that would definitely make her one of the 'in' people.

'Hey, Mazie, don't you get it? It's to actually protect you in case something really bad happens.'

Mazie agreed, assuming that she would then be given their passwords too. After all, wouldn't they want the same protection? She didn't mention that though. She just kept quiet after giving Holly her password.

Mazie felt a different sort of vibe at their next get-together. It wasn't something she could put a finger on; it just felt different. There was a look from one of the girls, a weird question out of the blue from another and then at one stage they had all run off, as if on some invisible cue, only to return a few moments later as if nothing had happened. Mazie said nothing; she was good at pretending nothing had happened. She didn't meet up with the girls the following afternoon after school. Instead she went to the local library. Amanda, a shy girl who had arrived at the start of term, had asked her a couple of times to visit the new library. She'd said that there was heaps of stuff to do there.

Mazie didn't see anyone she knew. She made her way over to a bank of computers and logged in. She was surprised to see so many messages in her inbox. She'd checked them after dinner the night before and her inbox had been empty.

As she read the first one, her stomach turned to jelly. Not only had it been sent to Mazie, it had also been sent to her entire friendship group. The words on the screen blurred as she fought back the tears. Beneath them was a picture of her from her Facebook profile that someone had photoshopped into a porn image. Underneath was written, 'Hey, call me...' with Mazie's number. Mazie felt like she was going to be sick. Quickly she shut down the computer and then raced out of the library, almost bumping into Amanda.

'Hey!' Amanda cried out, but Mazie just kept on running.

. . . .

This is a serious situation. The first step for Mazie to take is to tell a trusted adult (parent, school counsellor, adult family friend) about what has occurred. This will help Mazie deal with some of her strong feelings of guilt as she probably believes that she 'caused' this to happen.

She may also feel 'stuck' in that she doesn't know how to get out of the situation. It is also likely that Mazie is feeling sad and rejected by the group of people she thought were her friends. Counselling support is important to consider. Mazie shouldn't go it alone in this situation.

In terms of the nature of the cyberbullying, this is serious. Cyberbullying can occur at any time of the night or day and can be anonymous. Cyber images stay on the Internet for an indefinite length of time and can be sent to literally hundreds of thousands of people. The potential for significant psychological damage to the victim is high as they can be teased as long as the image is available (which can be forever) and by countless numbers of people.

Cyberbullying can be illegal. Different states in Australia have different rules so it is important to know what rules apply in your country. The Lawstuff website (*www.lawstuff. org.au*) has lots of cyberbullying information particular to each Australian state.

There is a Law in Victoria, Australia, called Brodie's Law which made bullying a crime. It was introduced after the suicide of a young woman called Brodie Panlock, who experienced significant bullying in her workplace.

Cyberbullying is a serious crime and the production and dissemination of cyberporn by underage people is also illegal.

As mentioned in Scenario #15, the Australian Government has established the Children's eSafety Commissioner, whose role it is to conduct investigations into cyberbullying. You can contact the Office of the Children's eSafety Commissioner by email: *enquiries@esafety.gov. au*, or telephone: *1800 880 176*.

So, after informing an adult, the next step Mazie could take is to ask the person who sent the email to recall the message from the inbox of the other people they sent it to. If this doesn't work, the next step is to report the bullying to the Children's eSafety Commissioner. Although this may feel like a big step, Mazie should feel proud that she is helping to get the message out to young people that cyberbullying and the production of underage porn is illegal and can have significant legal and psychological consequences for all involved.

KEEPING SAFE IN THE CYBER WORLD

★ It's really best to protect yourself in the first place. NEVER share your private information, such as passwords, your name, address or phone number, with people and especially people you don't know.

★ Block the sender and report them.

★ Find out how to report bullying and harassment on each of the different social networks that you use. Remember to set up the privacy options on your social networking sites in a way you are comfortable with.

★ Don't respond to messages when you are angry or hurt
– either to strangers or people that you know. This will
often encourage them to continue or increase their
harassment of you.

★ Keep a record of calls, messages, posts and emails that
may be hurtful or harmful to you.

★ **www.lawstuff.org.au/sa_law/topics/bullying/
cyber-bullying**: This site is run by the National
Children's and Youth Law Centre. It is an independent,
non-profit organisation working for and in support of
children and young people, their rights and access
to justice. The site has great information regarding
cyberbullying and also the laws that are applicable
in each state of Australia. The NCYLC also provides
advice and information about your legal rights and
responsibilities. They will advocate for you when your
rights or interests are threatened. They are on the
lookout to press for changes in the law and procedures
to better protect children from abuse and oppression.

★ **www.legalaid.vic.gov.au/find-legal-answers/sex-
and-law/resources/below-belt-sex-selfies-and-
cyberbullying**: Victoria Legal Aid has produced a
free Android phone app for young people. The App has
information about laws on sex and consent, sexting
and cyberbullying. You can use the app's tools to share
information with your friends or to obtain free or low-
cost help when you need it.

Key points to remember

Cyberbullying and cyberporn are serious issues – protect yourself in the first place.

There are some situations that you will need help to address – find a trusted adult.

Report any cyberbullying issues to the Office of the Children's eSafety Commissioner by email: *enquiries@ esafety.gov.au*, or telephone: *1800 880 176*.

#21

Liz – who suffers from constant pranks

Type: Covert

*'That's not really funny,' she scowled,
barging her way through the group.*

I can't even remember the first prank - they'd been going on and off for ages. I didn't really care that much in the beginning. I just pretended it was funny and laughed along with everyone else.

The week before, I couldn't find my sports uniform. Someone had taken it out of my sports bag and hidden it in the boys' changing rooms. Then on Wednesday of last week someone took my lunch from my bag. I don't know what they did with it. There were a few people standing around while I was scrounging through my bag. I thought maybe I'd forgotten to put my lunch in. They were laughing. I laughed along with them. I guess that's what friends did - it was just mucking around and it didn't happen every day. Luckily I had some money so it didn't really matter.

Last Friday I got the fright of my life. Someone had put a dead bird in my locker. It was gross. I screamed. Everyone came rushing over to see what had happened.

'Hey, Liz, you should look after your pet bird better,' said one of the boys, laughing. A few others joined in. I smiled, unsure what to say. Gabby came over though and gently picked up the bird in some tissues.

'That's not really funny,' she scowled, barging her way through the group. People moved out of her way. I was left standing there feeling a bit stupid. It was the first time that I started to feel angry as well. Why were my friends laughing all the time about these little jokes? Is that what friends did?

I didn't catch up with anyone over the weekend. To be honest I was feeling a bit scared suddenly about being with my friends. What would be the next trick they'd play on me? I needed to talk to someone, but who? I didn't want to bother my parents as they would start stressing as a few of my friends' parents were their friends too.

. . . .

What Liz has experienced is a perfect example of how pranks can turn into bullying situations. In general, pranks are thought of as harmless jokes or tricks that are lighthearted and not intended to cause any distress to anyone. However, although that may be the intention, often the outcome is not always positive, as Liz has experienced. If the prank is intended to embarrass, hurt or humiliate and if the person is clearly targeted, this is not harmless pranking... but bullying.

It appears that Liz has been singled out by a group of her friends and has been putting up with this for a long while. The fact that she feels humiliated and scared indicates that this is not just harmless fun. It's a clear indication that she is being bullied.

So the first step here is to recognise what is happening. Now that she can identify that she has been bullied over a long period of time, she may understand some of the feelings she has had. It may be that Liz feels 'different' and that she doesn't fit in with the group. She may also have a feeling of not being 'safe' and not knowing when and where the next bullying situation may happen.

It's not surprising that she doesn't want to catch up with people over the weekend; Liz doesn't know what might happen. On the other hand, her friendship group may have no idea of the emotional and psychological impact their 'pranks' are causing. They may see her as a popular member of the group, who is good humoured and easy going. This is because pranking is common and seen as being funny. As Liz is now aware, pranking is just as serious and causes the same emotional problems as overt bullying.

The most effective way to stop this happening to Liz would be for her to ask her friends to stop it. Make it simple, such as saying something like, 'Okay, guys, this was funny six months ago, but now I have had enough. Thanks.' Or, 'Do you think that was really funny?' Something to make them stop and allow them to think about what they are doing. Remember, they've been doing it for a long time.

Alternatively, Liz could let them know how she is feeling and educate them about what they are doing. 'Hey, guys, I have been feeling really bad about what has been happening and I've just found out that this is bullying.' Or, 'Agh, no wonder I'm feeling down. These aren't harmless pranks; it's in-your-face bullying.'

It would be good for Liz to have a closer look at her friendship group. Friends are there to support you, encourage you and make you feel good about yourself. This is not happening. It may well be that they are not aware of the impact of their bullying; however, it may be worthwhile for Liz to consider if these friends are the best she could have. It is not always easy changing friendship groups, but in the end she may be much better off.

Also worth noting is the positive behaviour Gabby displayed. She stopped playing the bystander role and stepped into the situation. She took the dead bird and said, 'That's not really funny.' She was assertive and her actions will also help break the cycle of the passive bystander role that so many people fall into, without really even knowing it. By standing by and doing nothing, you are actually condoning the bullying taking place.

Key points to remember

Recognise what is happening - pranks aren't funny; they're an example of bullying.

Trust your inner feelings; just because everyone else is taking it all in a lighthearted manner doesn't mean that you should also.

Let people know how you're feeling and tell them to stop their behaviour.

Evaluate your friendship groups - are these people really your friends?

#22

Petra – who is laughed at because of her cultural heritage

Type: Covert

This was going to be so embarrassing.

Petra was getting excited as next Saturday her whole family would visit and celebrate Slava together. Slava means 'celebration' and each year her family gather and bring with them traditional Serbian food and drink to honour their patron saint. Today Petra was going shopping with her mother to buy some of the food to make their traditional feast. She was looking forward to going to the Serbian deli to buy the pickled cabbage leaves and pork ribs for the Sarma dish. The smells in the deli were exciting...the salted fish and smoked meats.

Then Petra remembered that the deli was in the middle of town where some of the kids from school hang out. Of course they would comment on her being with her mother. They always did when they saw them together. And of course they would laugh at her going into the 'wog' deli. Petra laughed to herself when she thought of what they would say if they knew she was buying pickled cabbage leaves.

However, it didn't really make her feel any better about running into any of them.

Going into town with her mother made Petra feel embarrassed as her mother would often wear a big overcoat as she did in Serbia, even when it was summer. If she saw any of her Serbian friends they would laugh and talk very loudly in Serbian. This was going to be so embarrassing. Last time she was in town with her mother, the kids from school started to mimic her mother, laughing and gesturing with their hands. They even tried to imitate a Serbian accent.

Petra had the opportunity to talk with a couple of older friends from school whose opinions she valued and trusted. When she got home that night she jotted down her thoughts. Here are her thoughts after the chat she had.

. . . .

After chatting with Roma, Ben and Susie, I began to think of the importance of my family history and how excited I was that my whole extended family was coming to share Slava with me; well, with us! Really, the kids from school had no idea about my culture and family history. I guess the more I thought about it all, the more I realised just how proud I was of my family and I shouldn't feel embarrassed by them. We were a close, caring family who loved to eat and laugh together. My uncles had fought in the war. That, more than anything else, suddenly put things in perspective for me.

So I decided that I had better 'suck it up'. If my uncles fought in a war, then surely I could shop with my mother. Anyway I really loved helping her out with the shopping and cooking.

I thought out my plan. If the girls were in town then I'd just smile at them and keep walking. I'd hold my head up high, maybe even pretend to be slightly amused by them. I knew I would feel nervous, but I certainly wouldn't let it show.

I started to wonder just what it was that caused people to ridicule others who were culturally different. I guess I mean, why are they 'racist'? Perhaps they just take on the views of others around them or feel better when they hang out with people who are the same as them. If that's the case, they may see people who are different as a threat or perhaps they think that their ways are better.

I knew that the kids teased other people from different cultures, so it wasn't just about me. It was really about their lack of cultural awareness and not appreciating diversity. And then another thing struck me. The girls were never with their parents. I couldn't recall a time when I'd seen them shopping together. In fact they hardly mentioned their families at school. No, they were always hanging around on the street, sometimes being asked to move on by the police. They really didn't have a very good life at all. Shopping with Mum wasn't going to be for ever. Which was even more reason to enjoy it while I could.

Key points to remember

Find reasons to be proud of the person you are.

Have a plan to deal with bullying.

Hold your head up high and keep walking (a smile may help too!).

Sometimes bullying is not personal.

#23

Sally - who is taunted and teased on the bus

Type: Overt

Sally was pretty confident that they wouldn't do anything really violent, but still it was getting harder and harder to catch the bus.

Sally is thinking about avoiding going to school today. It's not that she doesn't like school or her bunch of new friends. It's the bus that's the problem. As soon as she gets on it she can feel the tension. The other kids on the bus are from the local high school and they fill up nearly the entire bus. Yesterday while she walked down the aisle looking for a spare seat the other students put their bags on them so she couldn't sit down. She ended up at the back of the bus and had to walk to the front again looking for a seat. It was so embarrassing. Sometimes they would comment on her uniform and how 'special' she must think she is. Last week one of them asked her why she couldn't catch the later bus. Why did she think she was welcome on this bus?

Yesterday she felt paper balls hitting her head from behind. Sally pretended to keep listening to her music, but really she was trying not to cry. It was obvious that the kids on the bus didn't like the school she went to. She knew it wasn't directly about her. Well at least she thought that was the case, though it still felt like a personal attack.

Sally was pretty confident that they wouldn't do anything really violent, but still it was getting harder and harder to catch the bus. It seemed to Sally that the worrying and thinking about being on the bus was nearly as bad as actually catching the bus and riding on it.

At night Sally thought about the kids and what they might do next. She pictured herself tripping as she walked down the aisle and then bursting into tears in front of them. The worrying about the next day was preventing her from sleeping, and feeling tired was making it all worse. She noticed too that her eating patterns were changing.

. . . .

It's time for Sally to tell someone what's going on. She could speak to her older sister or mum. If not, what about her sports coach? Or another trusted adult or friend from school? Or someone within her family? It's important that she thinks about who she can tell and feel confident that they will work with her in her best interest.

She may also be wondering why she can't deal with this herself. One of the outcomes of bullying is that you are made to feel disempowered. On the bus Sally is isolated from people that she knows and feels comfortable with.

Another reason why it's difficult to address these issues is the experience of feeling threatened and intimidated, which will make Sally too frightened to stand up to the bullies. Furthermore, the changes in her eating and sleeping habits and her crying are just normal responses to an abnormal situation.

There is nothing about Sally that is causing the problem and this is evidenced by the fact that she has a strong friendship group at school. The problem lies with the bullies and their belief that it is okay to intimidate and target someone.

Once Sally lets someone know what is happening there are various options she can take. Perhaps she could consider:

- ★ Sitting next to the driver - not cool, but it might work.

- ★ Going to school on a different bus.

- ★ Seeing if she can get a ride with another student from her school.

- ★ Riding to school - great for her general health and especially good to help with eating, sleeping and general feelings of anxiety.

- ★ Getting the school to contact the bus company and explain what's going on so they can monitor the students on the bus and take appropriate action. The bus company should have policies and procedures in place to deal with such issues, as should her school, and indeed the school that the troublemakers attend.

- ★ Sally's school can contact the bullies' school and request that they address the issues.

Sally doesn't deserve to be treated in this way; however, she may need to work with an adult to resolve this problem. Above all, Sally needs to do it now before she feels any worse.

Key points to remember

It helps a lot to tell a trusted friend or adult what is going on.

Bullying can affect our eating and sleeping patterns.

Develop strategies to deal with the situation if it appears to be ongoing.

Act sooner rather than later.

#24

Max – who is the butt of others' jokes and pranks

Type: Overt/Covert

I don't really talk with them;
they are not really my type.

I thought something was odd. There were no obvious signs, just these strange feelings I was having. Now that I think about it, they've been there for a while, I just hadn't realised. Well at least I think something is going on. Perhaps I'm just imagining everything or going crazy.

I remember last week in the gym. I turned round quickly to pick up my top and the boys were standing really close behind me. I hadn't noticed that they were there. When I turned around they just scattered and ran away. I thought perhaps a bell had gone and I didn't hear it.

The boys are in my class. I don't really talk with them; they are not really my type. My best friend is Adam. We get on really well together. He's not that keen on the other boys either. Another funny thing happened in class as well. The boys were sitting behind me, as they always seem to do. I could hear them sniggering and whispering, then I got a flash of their reflection in the window. They seemed to be pulling faces and it looked like they were pointing at me. Perhaps I was wrong, but that's what it looked like to me at the time.

I just don't know if this was really happening or whether I was imagining things. Maybe my anxiety is out of control. It makes me feel scared. I am not sure if what I'm seeing or feeling is real.

I wonder if the boys were also involved in sticking the post-it notes on my back. There was nothing written on them, just smiley faces, but when I took off my jumper there were about 10 notes stuck on me. I didn't even feel them. I don't understand why they would do that – did they think I would find it funny? Or am I some part of a joke? I don't understand what I could have done for them to be doing this to me.

I'm confused. Maybe I should see someone about my anxiety. Perhaps this is all related. Like it's a part of my unhelpful thinking processes, or perhaps I am really going crazy after all?

. . . .

This is not related to Max's anxiety – he is being bullied. This type of bullying can have a huge emotional impact. Recent research indicates that this type of bullying, known as covert bullying, has the potential to result in more severe psychological, social and emotional damage than schoolyard bullying that you can clearly observe.

So the first thing for Max to do here is to be fully aware of what is happening and clearly understand that how he is feeling is directly related to being bullied. His feelings are not an indication that he is emotionally or psychologically unwell and they are not directly related to his anxiety, although the bullying will add to his level of anxiety.

Max can ignore the boys; however they are getting their fun and encouragement from each other and not from his responses. Ignoring them won't have a significant effect on their behaviour. In this case it would be worthwhile for Max to let a teacher know what is happening and ask them how they can assist.

Schools have a duty of care to ensure that all students feel safe and to provide a supportive school environment. They also must take action to protect students from all forms of abuse. Max could suggest to his teacher or principal that he change classes so he can avoid the boys. He could also avoid them in the yard and where possible at sport. Perhaps Max could also suggest that the school develop programmes to inform teachers and students about all forms of bullying and how to increase positive relationships among students.

It's more than likely that other students are aware of what the boys are doing behind his back, so as bystanders they also have a role to play here in bully prevention. Often bystanders are not aware of how powerful they can be and they think they should 'stay out of it'. But a bystander who speaks out can have a significant impact on bullying behaviour. It would also be beneficial if the school raised awareness of the rights of students and the provision of their counselling and support structures, as it's likely that other students are also being affected and, like Max, are scared and confused.

The main aim here is for Max to let the school know what's going on and where possible remove himself from the bullies. This may also mean that he consider other schools. Above all, Max must not forget that his feelings and worries are a result of being bullied. There is nothing wrong with him.

Key points to remember

Some types of bullying are harder to detect. See page 13 to learn more about the different types of bullying.

Schools have a duty of care to protect students against bullying - ask to see your school's policy.

Tell a trusted teacher or school counsellor what's going on.

Bystanders are just as guilty as bullies.

It's okay to remove yourself from the situation.

#25

Steve – who is bullied because they identify as transgender

Type: Overt

'There goes the shemale.'

Even as a three-year-old, Steve asked his mum when he was going to grow into a girl. His mother just presumed this was a stage he was going through and didn't think much more of it, but Steve kept asking. As an eight-year-old, Steve would watch the girls in his class – how they walked, how they talked and how they did their hair. At home, in his bedroom, Steve would practise walking and talking like a girl. It made him feel good, as if he was 'at home in his own skin'. He even started to sneak into his parents' bedroom when they were not home and try on his mother's dresses, making sure to put them back exactly as he found them. He certainly didn't want his parents to know what he was doing and how normal it made him feel.

When Steve was in his early teens he was able to get a job delivering newspapers on his bike. He used the money he earned from his part-time job to buy make-up. He especially liked lipstick and nail polish, which he kept in the front of his school bag so his parents wouldn't find them. Steve had managed to keep his fascination with female clothes and make-up hidden from everyone, including his parents and, most importantly, the kids at school. Not that he had many friends at school. Most of the kids didn't really know him, and Steve kept to himself. There was one girl he would sometimes hang out with at lunchtime, but that was about it.

Steve felt that he was an imposter, having to dress up as a boy. He hated it when it came to team sports and he was forced to play football or when his class went to camp and he had to sleep and shower with the boys. Didn't they know he was a girl?

One day Steve was running late for the school bus. It was only when he hopped on board that he realised he hadn't taken off his nail polish from the night before!

'Oh no, this can't be happening,' he thought, reaching into his school bag and feeling around for some nail polish remover wipes, hoping to discreetly take the polish off while the bus was fairly quiet. But in his flustered state, he fumbled and the contents came tumbling out in full view of everyone. Steve's lipstick and nail polish rolled down the aisle. All Steve could do was to watch it happen in slow motion and try to hide his coloured nails.

'Is this yours, Steve?' asked Tim. Steve couldn't respond. 'You're a trannie!' yelled Hiran. The boys then started tossing Steve's make-up to each other and would not give it back to him. Steve just wanted to die. How could this be happening?

It wasn't long before all the kids at school knew what had happened on the bus. 'There goes the shemale.' 'Stay away from our loos, we don't want pervs in there.' 'Oooh, nice nails.' 'Give us a kiss, love.' And that was just the start.

. . . .

Adolescent transphobic bullying attacks the very essence of a person, often at the same time that the trans person is also coming to terms with their own gender identity. In the first instance it may be helpful remind yourself that transphobia and transphobic bullying is real, systemic and can be violent, so avoid places where you do not feel safe, and stay with a group of friends if possible so it's harder for you to be singled out.

It is important when you experience either face-to-face or online bullying that you don't react – that is just what the bully wants to see and it will reinforce their behaviour. Try to stay calm and walk away, or block them on social networks. Act confidently as if you don't really care what they think. You could even use humour – for example, if called names such as 'Shemale' you could respond with, 'How do you spell that?' It is also appropriate to tell them to stop doing what they are doing.

It is important that you seek support from someone you trust. Adolescence is in itself a difficult time; however, identifying yourself as being transgender and being bullied for being the person you are just adds to the complexities and problems. There are many wonderful online resources available as well as support groups you can join.

Don't blame yourself for the bullies' behaviour. It is a reflection of their lack of education about transgender people and their own biases and fear. Perhaps one of the ways of dealing with the bullying is to join a campaign to help educate people and support other transgender people. Look up all the information you can find on websites and with self-help groups, surround yourself with people who care and understand.

Key points to remember

Be true to yourself – you are okay in your own skin.

Where appropriate, be assertive and look the bully in the eye. Ask them to stop.

Keep yourself safe by staying away from areas where the bully might be.

Seek help from supportive people and surround yourself with those who care and understand.

Look up all the information you can find on websites and get advice from self-help groups.

Become empowered – start a campaign against transphobia!

Be(*you*)tiful.

#26

Brittany - who experiences homophobic bullying

Type: Overt/Cyber

I had been tagged with a homophobic meme that read, 'I am not afraid of gays... I just hate them.'

I've always thought I might be 'different', not feeling as if I fit. I can remember having 'strong' feelings for my Year 6 Physical Education teacher. I began to think that was odd, but justified it by knowing that I had strong feelings for my mother, and thought perhaps that was just a normal part of growing up. I had bits of feelings for other friends, but didn't really think much of it until I started secondary school and had a huge crush on one of the girls in the class. I was so shocked that I could have such strong feelings towards her. I thought everyone could actually see that I adored her. I watched her from afar and wished she would tell me that she felt the same...but it didn't happen. I was actually pleased that it didn't as I didn't want to feel this way. Gosh, what would my parents and my best friend, Fee, say? At that stage I tried to hide what was happening by talking about guys with my friends and how one day I was going to ask Jacob Jones for a date and we'd fall in love and live happily ever after... Who was I kidding!

I started to research homosexuality online, and fantasised that perhaps I was a lesbian...but no... I couldn't be... I wouldn't be. I dated a couple of boys, mainly to show others that I was 'normal'. But there was never any chemistry or real interest, especially after I had experienced my first crush on a girl. At the start of Year 10 I joined our local drama company and fell head over heels with one of the girls there. She was playing the lead role in the production. I hung on her every word, and followed her all around the set. After rehearsal one afternoon, we were putting the sets away and she came up and thanked me and touched my arm and smiled... Wow! After we'd finished, we sat in the green room talking about the production and opening night... We had a great conversation. We spoke for hours about life, our backgrounds, our friends and even the possibility that we had a special attraction for each other. I know I did!

I battled with the thought that perhaps I really was homosexual and what that would mean for my future; and on the other hand, how great it was to find a soul partner who understood me and what I had been going through, and also someone I admired and loved being with.

A few days later at Fee's house we were watching a movie (called *Bloomington*) about a student who became romantically involved with her female professor. Fee commented on how loving the two females were towards each other, as we discussed the storyline. This was my time... my time to let Fee know what I was experiencing and how I thought, well knew, that I was homosexual.

'Fee, I have something to tell you. I would have told you sooner but couldn't find the right time. I wasn't sure if it was true, but now I think it is. I have romantic feelings for my friend at acting class, who is a female.'

I should have guessed that Fee would not have understood at first. This was a new experience to me as well, even though I had been battling the feelings for a few years now. I was sure she would eventually understand and support me. Fee listened for a while and then said I should leave and that I was just trying to be trendy and cool, and she didn't expect that from me and I should grow up!

I was a bit surprised and taken aback by her response but sensed that to leave straight away was the best thing to do. Maybe she just needed a bit of time to digest it all. But I'd misread her completely.

The next day when I checked my Facebook and Instagram page, I found I had been tagged with a homophobic meme that read, 'I am not afraid of gays... I just hate them.' This was not just from Fee, but from a whole bunch of kids at school. It was out there! An hour later I opened up an email that chanted, 'Girl on girl...not welcome here' with a note below from Fee letting me know not to go near her again and to stay away from all of her female friends.

· · · · · · · · · · · · · ·

Stay strong! It's probably better that you don't respond to the bullies as this may add to their 'hate' and increase the frequency or even the intensity of their attacks. If you feel you have to respond, you could send a message that you don't care about what they say. Responding with something along the lines of, 'Thanks guys, you may not like me but I do, and I know plenty of other people who do too.' Or you could use some humour: 'Do you think I have time to read all of this stuff? At least one of us has a life.' Pretend you don't care and try to be assertive (the Assertiveness chapter on page 130 may help). Block the senders on social networks and inform the site moderator. This behaviour is not acceptable, nor is it in line with our rights as human beings.

It would also be helpful for you to speak with a person you trust and who understands what you are dealing with. There is also lots of good information on the Internet, including forums where people can share what they have experienced and how they handled the problem. A bit of research may also reveal the names of local support groups that may also be helpful. Schools are also mandated to provide a safe environment for students. Perhaps this situation is one a teacher may need to know about?

Key points to remember

Stay strong.

Don't respond to the senders. If you have to respond, use humour or a 'non-caring' attitude.

Block the people who are making the hurtful and unkind comments.

Talk to a person you trust about the situation.

Get more information and support via the Internet.

Sleeping

We know you've heard all this before, but teens and adolescents need huge amounts of sleep. The physical, emotional and hormonal changes taking place at this stage of life are profound. Poor, irregular, unsettled sleep can have really negative effects on a person's wellbeing, quite apart from their inability to function to the best of their ability - be it in the classroom, interacting with people or simply in a general sense in terms of functioning to the best of one's capability.

Here are some tips and pointers about getting a good night's sleep. Take on board some of the advice; experiment and see if removing one or more of the sleep blockers mentioned below actually makes a difference for you!

* Going to bed at the same time each night signals to your body that it's time to sleep.

* Finish exercising at least three hours before bedtime.

* Try and avoid drinking beverages with caffeine after 4pm.

* Avoid violent, scary or action movies or TV shows before bedtime. You could even download a relaxation app to help prepare yourself for a good night's sleep. This link might be useful: *mashable.com/2010/06/24/iphone-better-sleep*.

* People sleep best in dark rooms that are slightly cool.

* A bright light in the morning signals to your body that it's time to get moving.

* Train your body and brain to build connections between bed and sleep – it's better to avoid watching TV or playing computer games in bed.

* Ever noticed how problems and worries seem to grow large and sometimes even become a little overwhelming at night? There are no 'real-time' points of reference to help us get a balance and perspective... so the worries escalate and keep us awake!

* Don't bring your problems to bed – try and sort them in some way before you climb into the cot. Jot them down, come up with a plan of action and look for some resolution to the day.

* Learn some relaxation techniques to help drift your mind away to a sleepy place.

* If you find it hard to stop thinking, then at least make sure you're thinking about fun, pleasant, lovely things.

* Try and get the family to establish some relaxing pre-sleep rituals – remember bedtime stories?

* Light signals the brain to wake up. Staying away from bright lights (including computer screens!) can help your body relax. It is good practice not to use computers, TV and phones at least one hour before you go to bed.

Make your bedroom a screen-free zone. Switch off the world and give your body the best possible chance to recuperate from the day just gone and prepare for the next one to come.

FURTHER READING

'**Teenage sleep: Understanding and helping the sleep of 12-20-year-olds,**' **by Dorothy Bruck:** This is a comprehensive e-book about teenage sleep and can be downloaded from:

http://eprints.vu.edu.au/467

National Sleep Foundation: The National Sleep Foundation is dedicated to improving the quality of life for people who suffer from sleep problems and disorders. They help people better understand the importance of sleep and the benefits of good sleep habits, as well as help you recognise the signs of sleep problems so that they can be properly diagnosed and treated.

www.sleepfoundation.org

Australasian Sleep Association: The mission of the Australasian Sleep Association (ASA) is to promote and foster professional education, training and research in sleep health and sleep science, advance the professional interests of its members, establish clinical standards with the profession and industry and be the recognised voice of sleep research and clinical expertise.

www.sleep.org.au

Anxiety

Anxiety is like feeling nervous and scared. It happens to everyone when they feel they are in danger or if they are overly worrying about something. In fact, it can be a normal response to an abnormal situation. Sometimes anxiety is good as it sparks us up and gets us going. At other times, however, high anxiety can prevent us from doing anything, or at least from doing those things well or to a standard we are capable of.

Anxiety affects us in three ways: in how we think, in what we do, and in our body's physiological response. When we are anxious our body speeds up and prepares us for action. So the heart beats faster, we breathe more rapidly, we can start to sweat, we can feel shaky and we may have an urgent desire to go to the toilet - in general we feel physically stressed. Sometimes our brains slow down and so thinking clearly can be difficult - which adds to the problem.

When we are feeling this way physically, we can often panic and our thinking can be quite negative. We can tell ourselves unhelpful and unrealistic thoughts such as, 'I am going to pass out if I have to walk past that bully,' or 'If I go to school, I will make a fool of myself.'

As an end result, our behaviour changes and we avoid what we are worrying about or try to leave as soon as we can. Some people develop complex avoidance strategies, telling their parents that they are ill (which in fact they may be feeling due to the anxiety), or hiding in the toilets at school to avoid someone.

Anxiety is maintained when you go along with your avoidance behaviour and negative thinking and do not try to address the concern or fear. That is why one of the main messages of this book is to 'TAKE CONTROL'.

So what can you do about it?

One of the easiest ways to address the physical symptoms of anxiety is to teach your body to relax. The most common way is called 'progressive muscle relaxation', which just means focusing on each of the muscle groups in the body and allowing them to relax. Turn to page 133 for a great muscle relaxation exercise. Remember the body can't be stressed and relaxed at the same time. Another useful strategy is to control your breathing. When we are nervous we often take short, shallow breaths that add to the bad physical feelings. You can find out more about controlled breathing by looking at page 134.

Now to your thinking. Really, it's all in the thinking, or what you tell yourself. Reflect on what you are saying to yourself and how realistic it is. It is often the negative thinking leading up to an event that causes the problem, not the event itself - test it out. Next time you are a little worried about something that is coming up, write down what you are telling yourself about the event. Is what you are telling yourself really likely to happen? Another question you could ask yourself is, 'Is there anything I could do to improve the outcome?' Or alternatively, visualise yourself as being assertive and in control, with the event having a positive outcome. (Refer to page 130 for more information.)

Currently there are two main ways to deal with our thinking. One is to challenge our negative thinking and replace it with more positive and realistic thinking. The second way is to accept our thinking as being irrational and then work on strategies to ignore that thinking.

There is a lot of good information on the web regarding these two approaches, but it is always better to work with someone who is skilled in these areas and who can guide you through the process.

The final thing to do is...actually DO IT! Stop the avoiding, take that deep breath, lift up your head and go for it. You may not feel confident inside, but outside you will look like a tower of strength.

And you will be facing your fears!

Nutrition

It's a multi-billion dollar industry that churns out hundreds of books every year. You'd think by now we'd have all the answers to the whole nutrition/diet/food dilemma... Alas, no. Along with good sleeping and good exercise, good nutrition is one of the most important things you can control to enjoy a happy and healthy life. The key word is moderation. Michael Pollen, who wrote *The Omnivore's Dilemma* (2006), delivers the message in seven words: 'Eat food. Not too much. Mostly plants.' By food, he is referring to real food, a throwback to the days before processing swamped the food industry.

We're sure you've been bombarded with healthy eating tips from an early age - as much perhaps as you've been bombarded with advertisements for processed and fast food. Here are some great nutrition tips that WILL make a difference. Remember, we're not suggesting that every breakfast now should be a pureed raw egg and carrot smoothie and that you never eat fast food again, let alone look at it! It's all about balance and timing. Balance is that you don't overeat or overindulge in one particular food or food group

- especially if it's a food that has limited nutritional value. Timing is all about when you eat. Breakfast, to literally break the fast that you've endured by sleeping the past eight hours, is a very important meal. It energises the body and brain with fuel to prepare you for the busy day ahead.

Teenagers are at a vulnerable age, as they are so open to what the media and their peers are saying and doing in all manner of things and especially things related to food. But it's also the time when the body is growing rapidly and needs good nutrition to support this growth spurt.

A diet high in fat (especially saturated fat), salt and sugar, or foods low in fibre and nutrients (like calcium and iron) can lead to all sorts of problems even at this tender age. Some of these potential issues are:

* becoming overweight

* heart problems

* constipation

* higher blood pressure

* tiredness

* concentration issues.

So, how well do you perform when it comes to healthy eating? Give yourself a score from one to five for the following. Better still, do it yourself, *and then* get someone who knows you (very) well to score you. Average the two sets of scores for perhaps a more accurate rating.

1 = never / 2 = occasionally / 3 = usually / 4 = often / 5 = always

Eating at least five servings of vegetables and two servings of fruit a day - preferably they have different colours, so we're not talking about five carrots!

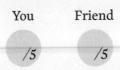

You   Friend

/5   /5

Eat breakfast.

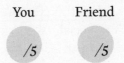

You   Friend

/5   /5

Drink at least four glasses of water every day.

You   Friend

/5   /5

Have fewer than two fizzy drinks per week.

You   Friend

/5   /5

Have 'fast food' once a week or less.

You   Friend

/5   /5

Have fruit and healthy snack options and actually eat them when feeling hungry.

You   Friend

/5   /5

Be involved in the cooking process at least a couple of times a week.

You	Friend
/5	/5

Be conscious and proactive about ensuring that you have moderate-sized portions of food on your plate.

You	Friend
/5	/5

Eat your meal slowly, with others at a table, and enjoy the experience of eating food that tastes good.

You	Friend
/5	/5

Total scores

You	Friend
/45	/45

Your average score

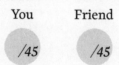

You

/45

Over 36 - You're doing extremely well - keep it up!

30-35 - There's room for improvement but it sounds like you have good nutritional habits.

22-29 - It looks like there are some areas for you to improve on with regards to nutrition so start writing down some goals for yourself to improve your eating habits. You are more likely to achieve small goals so don't go cold turkey and decide that you'll live off lettuce leaves and goat's cheese.

Below 22 - Well, if nothing else you (or your friend!) have been very honest, so that's a start. But seize the moment now and make a conscious decision by telling yourself that the time has come to make a change. It doesn't have to be a big change; more than likely nothing will change if you set your goals too high. But write down some goals, tell them to a friend and make a commitment to improve your eating habits.

Exercise

The importance of physical exercise for people of all ages cannot be underestimated. Apart from the obvious physical and health benefits (less cardiovascular risk, better bone mass, leaner body mass, etc.) there are enormous mental wellbeing and social benefits for people who can manage some form of daily regular exercise.

Here, we are more interested in the benefits of exercise to healthy and happy living. One of the very positive aspects of physical exercise is the sense of personal satisfaction it can generate. If you're feeling lethargic, moody, tired or irritable put on the joggers, the bike helmet, the bathers or just wrap yourself in a warm coat and get outside and walk - hard! The harder the better. It seems to be a contradiction, but physical exercise will energise you, blow out the cobwebs and clear the head. It is cheap, in the moment and at your doorstep. The hardest part, of course, is getting out of the chair and to the door, but you won't regret the 20 (or more!) minutes you give to your body - and mind.

It is true to say that the less you do, in terms of physical activity, the more likely it is that you will be moody, tense and worried. Here are some known benefits of exercise.

★ You'll be less likely to experience depression.

★ Your levels of anxiety and stress will be diminished.

★ You'll be able to concentrate better.

★ You'll be more likely to sleep better.

★ You'll be better able to cope with cravings or withdrawal symptoms.

Okay, so you grudgingly agree that this is all making sense. 'How much do I have to do?' you ask. Well, some exercise is better than none, of course, and actually it only needs to be a moderate amount. How does 4–5 times a week with about 30 minutes of exercise on each occasion sound? You can break up the 30-minute session into a morning 15 minutes and afternoon 15 minutes if that suits you better. Ideally, small amounts of exercise often is better than one gut-busting 70-minute workout once a week. Start small too, building up a regime in small steps.

Here are some ideas – maybe one or more will work for you. A 40-minute jog by yourself is not for everyone; nor is a pump class at the end of the day with music blasting! But you need to make the effort to find what works for you. Try and establish a routine. Keep an exercise diary. Set some goals. Reward yourself if you achieve your goals.

★ **Park Run:** This is an ever-growing 5 km running event that is happening in more and more towns around the world. Check out *www.parkrun.com.au* to find an event nearest to you. It's free, relying totally on volunteers. Being able to run non-stop for 5 km is a fantastic goal to work towards. If you can do that, then start thinking about setting some goals in terms of your times. If there's not a Park Run event near you, then get in touch with the organisers and start one! What a brilliant thing to do for your local community.

* **Couch to 5 km:** Okay, so maybe the Park Run idea was a little intense for you. Maybe you're a person who would find it a challenge to run to the end of the street! No problems. Try the Couch to 5K app (C25K). It's designed to get almost anyone off the couch and onto the road. It has a clever structure that is designed to keep you on track for the full nine-week journey. Follow the programme and you will be running for 30 minutes over a 5 km course without stopping!

* **Hit the gym:** It's loud, noisy and a great way to meet people. One of the advantages of doing gym sessions (class or personalised workouts) is that you're paying for the weekly, monthly or yearly plan and of course you don't want to waste your money by too many no-shows! So if you think you'll find the whole motivation thing a problem, then this could be a great option for you.

* **Walking:** Free, cheap and super easy. But don't stroll. Go hard. Pop in the earplugs (not too loud so you can't hear the traffic) set up a 30-minute playlist and see how far you can go. Don't worry about carrying weights or swinging your arms about; just walk fast. Get up a little sweat. Get the heart pumping blood through all your large muscles. One of the great benefits of cardiovascular exercise is that when you're done and sitting back on the couch, your body isn't. The heart is still pumping faster than normal so you're burning the kilojoules at a higher rate than you would had you never left the couch.

* **Cycling:** This is definitely money well spent. It's a challenge for some in the winter months and riding 80 km on the fringe of a busy road may not be for you, but more and more bike lanes and tracks are appearing. Work out a circuit and go pedalling.

★ **Clubbing!** One of the great benefits of getting involved in a sporting club is the social element. Most are open to a variety of ages, some are seasonal, but all have their own appeal. If children are given the chance to be involved in these sporting communities, there's a greater chance that they will be able to manage leisure time in later life in a positive way. There are many opportunities for volunteers also, so it can become a family commitment too. Here are some sports and activities that may be available near you:

- Aerobics
- American football
- Athletics
- Australian rules football
- Baseball
- Canoeing
- Cricket
- Cycling
- Dancing – a variety of styles!
- Dragon boat racing
- Futsal
- Gymnastics
- Hockey
- Indoor cricket
- Mountain biking
- Rowing
- Rugby – league or union
- Running – various club/groups/events
- Sailing
- Soccer
- Softball
- Surf lifesaving
- Swimming
- Table tennis
- Tennis
- Triathlon
- Walking
- Wall/rock climbing

Assertiveness

Assertiveness is a learned skill and, like any other skill, it takes time to master. Some suggestions you might consider are:

* Decide that you want to be assertive rather than aggressive or passive.

* Practise talking in an assertive way, alone or with a friend.

* Respect the needs and feelings of others - accept that their viewpoint may be different to yours.

* Take a problem-solving approach to conflict and try to see the other person as your partner rather than your opposition.

* Tell the other person honestly how you feel without making accusations or trying to make them feel guilty.

* If the exchange doesn't go well, learn from the experience and plan how you will do things a little differently next time.

ASSERTIVENESS TIPS

Use body language

* Look the person in the eye.

* Hold your body upright.

* Consciously relax your shoulders.

* Try to breathe normally and don't hold your breath.

* Keep your face relaxed.

Watch your language

* Speak at a normal conversational volume (don't yell or whisper).

* Use assertive language such as 'I feel', 'I perceive' or 'I believe', rather than aggressive language such as 'You always' or 'You never'.

* Don't interrupt the other person when they are talking, and try hard to listen and understand their point of view.

* If you feel the other person is behaving as though you are having an argument, try not to get emotionally involved; keep your head and your sense of perspective. Try to stay rational. Tell the person you'll take up the subject again at another time and then leave.

* If you decide to stick it out, remain calm. Steer the conversation back to the original point and try to understand the other person's point of view.

* Appreciate that there may be other issues motivating their behaviour.

* Don't take heat-of-the-moment criticisms to heart.

Meditation and Relaxation

It's not for everyone but this is definitely worth a try. If nothing else, you get a little break in the day from the hustle and bustle of living. Think of it like a pit stop in a car race. You're off the track for a little while, out of the race so to speak, but after a short moment you're back in play - energised, revitalised and ready to surge on...

Meditation for 20-30 minutes per day can benefit people by:

★ reducing generalised anxiety

★ preventing stress build-up

★ increasing energy and productivity

★ improving concentration and memory

★ reducing insomnia and fatigue

★ preventing and reducing psychosomatic disorders such as hypertension, migraines, headaches, asthma, and ulcers

★ increasing self-confidence and reducing self-blame

★ increasing the availability of feelings.

There are different forms of relaxation techniques, including autohypnosis, progressive muscle relaxation, and many forms of yoga, to mention a few.

Below is an easy relaxation procedure, which combines several aspects of these approaches.

* Start by seating yourself in a comfortable position in a quiet area. Loosen your clothing so that you do not feel constricted in any way.

* Close your eyes. Progressively move from one muscle group to another: face, neck, shoulders, arms, fists, chest, back, buttocks, thighs, calves and feet.

* Tighten each in turn and then relax. Feel the contrast between the tight experience and the relaxed experience. Notice the tingling or whatever sensation you have.

* Just notice it; don't do anything about it.

* As you relax each area, focus on your breathing. Breathe slowly and rhythmically until your entire body relaxes.

* Finally, imagine yourself in a location that you find especially relaxing, safe and comfortable. For some people this might be a secluded beach, for others a mountain lake. Each of us has our own place. Discover your own place - one that you'll return to often.

* Once you have the image in mind, make it as clear as you can, almost as though you are there. Let your thoughts go - don't try to capture them or block them; just let them drift by.

* Stay in your 'place' for 5-10 minutes and then slowly and quietly remind yourself to come back to your present time or place.

* Gently open your eyes and gradually reorient yourself. This approach takes about 15-20 minutes. You should feel refreshed when you are finished.

DIAPHRAGMATIC BREATHING

Like meditation, good breathing can have a really positive effect on your physical and mental wellbeing. Good diaphragm breathing reduces stress, increases the oxygen to your muscles and brain, and has a general calming effect. Actually, it can be an immediate stress reliever. In a moment of panic and stress, we often find ourselves breathing in a shallow and strained manner. Getting the diaphragm involved is a great countermeasure. The diaphragm is a big muscle just below your lungs. A good breath means the lungs expand and push down on the diaphragm, which in turn expands the abdomen.

Here's how to do it:

* Place one hand on the abdomen and the other on your upper chest.

* If you do a diaphragmatic breath, you should feel the lower hand on your abdomen move out with the inhalation and in with the exhalation.

* The top hand on the chest should remain relatively still. If you find it hard to do sitting down, then try lying on the floor.

* Try to sigh slightly with your exhalation as this can provide extra tension relief.

* The inhale stimulates the sympathetic nervous system, and when you exhale it stimulates the parasympathetic nervous system. So put more emphasis on exhaling for a little longer than inhaling.

* Focus on breathing rhythmically rather than deeply.

Self-Talk

How we deal with a situation is often dictated by what we tell ourselves about what is happening or how we talk to ourselves.

Self-talk is the mental communication we have with ourselves. How we speak to ourselves and what we tell ourselves has a direct impact on our feelings. Sometimes we can make ourselves feel really bad even if the actual situation is not really so terrible. If we tell ourselves that 'we are not good enough' or that 'we can't do it', it is certain that we will feel negative towards ourselves, self-defeating and perhaps even anxious about new experiences. When we feel this way, we find ways of discouraging ourselves or avoid taking any action. On the other hand, if we say to ourselves 'I will give it a go' or 'I will do my best', it is likely that we will feel better about ourselves and more prepared to try new things.

Self-talk is very powerful, as what we tell ourselves and how we feel about what we say sends a chemical message to our brain just like if we were actually in that same situation. For example, if we say, 'I am hopeless, I can't meet new people as I get really anxious,' the brain sends messages to our body to respond and prepare. We breathe faster, we might start sweating and feeling uncomfortable, our stomach might tighten and adrenalin clouds our thinking. Such negative thinking creates real stress in our mind and body.

The first thing to do is to become more aware of what you are telling yourself, to listen to your inner dialogue. Then start changing your negative talk to a more positive type of self-communication.

Carefully choose the words you want to use. It is best to use them in the present tense. For example, instead of saying, 'I will try to be a better friend,' say 'I am a great friend.' Talk to yourself the way you want to be.

Focus on the solution, not the problem – look at what you can do. For example, if you are being picked on or teased, don't dwell on what is happening. Rather, look forward to what you can do to address it: 'I know this is happening and I can do this to change it.'

Be careful if your self-talk contains lots of 'shoulds' or 'always'. For example, instead of saying, 'I always mess things up,' change it to 'I made a mistake this time and this is what I can do to change it.' Being aware of our self-talk and changing it to a more positive communication takes time and practice. Your school counsellor is a great resource for more information and support. The following web links may also be useful:

★ **http://au.reachout.com/What-is-self-talk**: ReachOut.com is Australia's leading online youth mental health service. Here you can get the help you need, where and when you need it. Every year ReachOut.com helps hundreds of thousands of people under 25 tackle everything from finding motivation to getting through really tough times. You can access ReachOut.com no matter where you are. With tools and tips for making everyday life a little easier, it's the perfect place to start if you don't know where to look.

* **http://headspace.org.au/get-info/tips-for-a-healthy-headspace:** Headspace is the National Youth Mental Health Foundation. They help young people who are going through a tough time. Their site has lots of well-researched and practical information and resources and is well worth a visit.

So You Think You're a Bully?

It is not always easy to examine our own behaviour to determine whether we are capable of bullying, but if you can answer 'yes' to any of the questions below, the chances are that you need to start changing how you relate to people.

★ Do you play practical jokes where the person is left feeling embarrassed or physically hurt?

★ Do you target people just for the sake of upsetting them? Either face-to-face or online?

★ Do you tease someone on a regular basis?

★ Are you part of a group that teases others?

★ Do you like making people do what you want to do?

★ Have you pushed someone around?

★ Do you spread rumours about other people?

★ Do you ridicule someone to try to make your friends laugh?

Sometimes people think that bullying is just harmless teasing, but it's not... Bullying can affect people's self-esteem, confidence, education and ultimately their lives.

Also, other people usually don't like someone who bullies, even though they pretend to like the person doing the bullying.

WHAT CAN THE BULLY DO?

It is important to understand that the bully can change once they are aware that the behaviour is hurtful and that they can take control to stop hurting other people. The bully needs to think about why they behave the way they do to others. It might be because that's how people in their family relate to each other. Or perhaps someone treats them in a similar way and they are imitating a behaviour they have come to know as normal. Or maybe it makes them feel better about themselves?

Whatever the reason, the bully needs to reflect on and change their behaviour. It is possible that the bully lacks the ability to feel empathy. A reason why so many bullies stop bullying is because they learn the effect their words, actions, etc. have on other people.

It would be beneficial for the bully to apologise to the person hurt. This could be face-to-face or in a letter. Apologising could be the first step for the bully to make some positive changes and also a big help to the person who has been hurt as they can also start to heal and move on. The bully could seek out a friend they feel comfortable confiding in to gain their support to assist them in changing their behaviour.

Involving a friend or family member might encourage the bully to be more accountable in terms of committing to altering their bullying ways.

Being able to pause for a moment before speaking or acting can often be all that is needed to stop the words being said.

Harsh words are like toothpaste coming out of a tube. Easy to put out there but very hard to put back! Developing the habit of pausing and thinking a little before speaking is a good skill to work on.

Keeping oneself busy and active is another positive step a bully can take. Being involved in sport, especially team-oriented games, is another worthwhile consideration. It would give the bully the chance to interact with others in a positive and supportive manner, and ideally expose them to positive role models.

No one is asking the bully to like everyone they meet. But there should be an expectation that they always interact with others in a respectful manner. This expectation should be one that siblings, parents, classmates, friends, teachers and members of the wider community demand of the people in their world.

Above all, the bully needs to be responsible for their behaviour, admit to themselves what they are doing, and start relating to others in a respectful, caring, empathetic way.

Bullying in Schools

Bullying occurs in some form or another in most, if not all, schools.

Most schools are proactive about dealing with the problem and commit to some or all of the following:

* building a community of tolerance and respect

* offering programmes for students that promote ideals of self- esteem, responsibility, respect and empathy

* through questionnaires and surveys, giving students the opportunity to identify students who bully

* ensuring that their parents have the opportunity to be involved in a programme by way of information evenings and communicating the school's ideals, values and goals via information bulletins and the like

* ensuring there are clear, purposeful guidelines and structures in place to deal with bullying situations

* ensuring the appropriate level of teacher supervision is taking place in all areas of the school and at all times the school gates are open.

One of the best things a school can do in the first instance is to make an honest and open assessment about how well the school is maintaining a safe and supportive learning environment. The National Safe Schools Framework has an audit tool designed to do just that (https://school-audit-tool.studentwellbeinghub.edu.au).[1]

The authors of the Audit have identified nine categories in a school that would have an impact on its ability to provide such an environment:

1. Leadership commitment to a safe school.

2. A supportive and connected school culture.

3. Policies and procedures.

4. Professional learning.

5. Positive behaviour management.

6. Engagement, skill development and safe school curriculum.

7. A focus on student wellbeing and student ownership.

8. Early intervention and targeted support.

9. Partnerships with families and community.

Four rating scales are used to allow for stakeholders to indicate the level of truth they feel applies to a number of statements within each variable or category. The rating scales are:

1. Definitely true.

2. Mostly true.

3. Only true to some degree.

4. Not true.

---

1 Please note that permission has been given for the use of various sections of the National Safe Schools Framework Resource Manual.

STEPS TO DEVELOP A SAFE AND SUPPORTIVE SCHOOL PLAN

Step 1
Complete the school audit.

Step 2
Identify the characteristics of the nine elements that your school is already addressing well.

Step 3
Identify the gaps in the nine elements that your school still needs to work on.

Step 4
For information about implementing strategies to address areas of concern in your school, visit *www. safeschoolshub.edu.au/safe-schools-toolkit/overview*.

Step 5
Document your safe school policies and practice. This process could involve the broader school community.

Step 6
Promote how your school is safe and supportive to the whole school community.

Step 7
Repeat the audit every 12 months and build on your good practice.

Having studied a number of reviews and procedures, certain elements have been consistently evident in schools where less bullying occurs. These are:

* a universal whole-school approach of long duration that takes a multi-faceted approach rather than focusing on one single component

* an increased awareness of bullying in the school community through assemblies, focus days and student-owned plans and activities

* a whole-school detailed policy that addresses bullying

* effective classroom management and classroom rules

* the promotion of a positive school environment that provides safety, security and support for students and promotes positive relationships and student wellbeing

* effective methods of behaviour management that are consistently used, are non-hostile and non-punitive

* encouragement and skill development for all students (and especially bystanders) to respond negatively to bullying behaviour and support students who are bullied

* social skill development within teaching and learning activities (e.g. through the use of cooperative learning)

* enhancement of the school physical environment and its supervision

* teacher professional development and classroom curriculum units that address bullying and related issues (e.g. values education)

* counselling for individual students and collaboration with other appropriate professionals

* school conferences or assemblies that raise awareness of the problem

* parent partnerships and education.

Additional evidence-informed approaches that have been identified as having significant potential include:

* addressing boredom and disengagement both in class and the playground

* values education with a focus on respect for the rights and feelings of others, acceptance of diversity, compassion, fairness, cooperation and inclusion

* the use of the *Method of Shared Concern* or the *Support Group Approach*

* the use of the *Restorative Practices* approach

* the use of *Positive Behaviour Support*

* the use of 'social architecture' (i.e. redesigning students' social interactions and facilitating social opportunities within a class or year-level context)

* early intervention with students identified as being at-risk for bullying others or being bullied in order to provide them with developmental support.

Every person in a school community, regardless of their role, needs to actively demonstrate appropriate interpersonal communication. Be it teacher to student, parent to parent, parent to student, teacher to teacher, etc., the school needs to build a culture of positive relationships between every person who forms a part of the whole. And every one of those people who represent the whole school community needs to make a commitment that as a responsible member of that community, they will adhere to the school's guidelines at all times with regard to the way they interact with everybody else.

A Note for Parents

You can play a vital role in preventing your child from being bullied or bullying other children. What you model as a parent has a significant influence on the social behaviour of your child. If children are exposed to parents or family members whose only method of dealing with conflict is to use physical force, ridicule or personal power over someone else, that is how the child will deal with issues in their own social jungle. Parenting styles can affect how a child will interact with peers. Parents who have strict rules and expectations, who do not explain why rules are important, who punish their child when they do not obey the rules and do not give the child options and choices are more likely to have a child who is more aggressive outside of the home, has social difficulties and a lowered self-esteem.

PREVENTION

It is essential that you teach your child the various ways that problems can be solved rationally. It's important that you explain to your child why some rules are important and discuss with them why that might be the case. Give your child positive feedback when they behave well in a social situation – this helps to build up their social self-confidence. Talk about social situations and related problems and discuss how you might address them. You could talk about situations that arose when you were at school, the issues you had to deal with and the choices you made at the time and more helpful choices you would make now. You could even talk about social situations at work, how you feel about them and what you did.

Let your child know that social problems are common, they carry with them emotional pain and that you too have to navigate the social jungle on occasions. This allows your child to develop several strategies or 'tools in their back pocket' to address social problems such as bullying. The more responses your child has to choose from, the better prepared they will be to successfully manage social issues.

It's also essential that your child develops empathy and acceptance of difference. Be a good example to your child – when talking with people, be respectful and thankful. Talk to your child about what it might feel like to be bullied. Discuss current events that require acceptance of another culture or physical ability. There are also some great story books you can read to your child about overcoming bullying. Ask at your child's school, the local library or bookshop.

Model confident behaviour. Teach your child to be assertive; perhaps even role play a situation using the following statements: 'I want you to call me by my proper name'; 'There is no need to speak to me like that'; 'I want you to stop what you are doing'; 'I'm going to ignore that comment'. Point out to your child that they need to be where bullies aren't. Bullies are not usually around adults, so let your child know that it is okay to sit at the front of the bus, or to play in open supervised areas. Avoidance is also a good strategy.

WHEN TO WORRY

Children who are either bullies or victims often display various emotional or behavioural warning signs such as:

* withdrawal

* school avoidance

* drop in academic performance

* avoidance of social situations, which in turn can lead to a loss of friends

* a loss of interest in activities they used to enjoy doing

* they may also have torn clothing, bruising or even ask for extra money to 'negotiate' with the bully.

WHAT TO DO

* Believe your child if they say they are being bullied and 'be on their side'.

* Discuss strategies to address the situation - not physical retaliation.

* Talk to the child's teacher and if they don't stop the situation speak to the principal.

* Work with the school and continue to work until the bullying has stopped.

* Seek advice and support for your child and yourself from the school counsellor.

* If concerned about cyberbullying, contact the Office of the Children's eSafety Commissioner by email: *enquiries@ esafety.gov.au*, or telephone: *1800 880 176*.

Parents can play a significant role in the prevention of bullying by providing a caring, loving and safe environment and being there for their child to guide them through the bullying situation.

Check out the following:

* **www.stopbullying.gov/what-you-can-do/parents:** Stop bullying is an American Government website managed by the US Department of Health and Human Services. It has lots of information for parents, teachers, teenagers and the community. Some great resources too!

* **http://raisingchildren.net.au:** This site is a great resource with lots of up-to-date and relevant articles for parenting newborns to teens.

Moving On

LIFE DOESN'T COME WITH A SET OF RULES

Hopefully you will have realised that this is not just a book about deterring or stopping bullies. It doesn't set out to provide step-by-step instructions for the reader - if only life was that easy! Life is full of wrongs that may never be made right; however, life is too short and important to keep focusing on what has gone wrong...and at some stage you need to let go and move on.

Remember, the bullying was the other person's behaviour, not yours. We can't change other people. But we can control our own thinking and self-talk.

Take care of your health - eat well, develop a regular sleeping pattern and try to get in some daily exercise. Be aware of your mental health, and if you're 'just not feeling right', seek help. Act assertively. Sometimes how we behave becomes how we feel. You can portray an air of confidence, which could thus act as a possible deterrent to bullies, such as:

* holding your head back, walking tall and with purpose and confidence and wearing a face of calmness and confidence

* using an even, level and almost neutral voice when communicating rather than an emotional, whiney or aggressive voice.

You may even consider forgiveness. Forgiveness does not mean that the bully will change, or that you have to like them. It means that you can start to let go. Forgiveness requires compassion, understanding that the person who bullied you is human and due to some failing in themselves they made a poor choice. It also doesn't mean they are exempt from moral responsibility for their actions. It means only that we understand they were not acting as 'monsters', but as humans. And on occasions, humans do stuff up.

What is required is for you to think about how best you can apply the range of strategies suggested throughout the book so that they work for you. It's also about making changes so that you are better able to deal with bullying situations when they arise. Whether you're the target of the bullying, a bystander, a parent or teacher, being able to identify the most appropriate strategy to use and then apply it with confidence, conviction and resolution will increase the chances that you can deal with the bullying with strength and character.

It's about *you*, not the bully. It's about you being true to yourself and the values you stand for. It's about identifying those values and holding them firm. Bullying is a time when you'll be tried and tested. See this as your moment to stand tall and be the person you aspire to be. See it as an opportunity. A chance to show yourself, your family and friends, and the bully too, the person you are.

Ultimately, we as individuals must take responsibility for managing our lives. The sooner you start doing this, the sooner you'll be able to break free from the anxieties and hurt that the bully tries to inflict on you. Bullying is all about power. Don't let what has happened to you define you as a person. It's time for you to take back control.

Further Information

AUSTRALIA

Beacon

Provides consumers and professionals with information about e-health online applications for mental health and physical health disorders. Websites throughout the world are reviewed and ranked by a panel of health researchers. Consumers are invited to submit rankings and comments. Participation is free and anonymous.

www.beacon.anu.edu.au

beyondblue

beyondblue is a comprehensive site that provides real-time support, a huge range of resources, facts about a range of issues including depression, anxiety and various forms of treatment. There are forums, personal stories and the opportunity for people to get involved in a variety of ways to improve the mental wellbeing of people of all ages.

www.beyondblue.org.au

Black Dog Institute

The Black Dog Institute website contains:

- ⋆ expert information on depression and bipolar disorder
- ⋆ information about causes and treatments
- ⋆ online self-assessment tools
- ⋆ a section on getting help for people experiencing depression
- ⋆ a section about depression in teenagers and young adults.

www.blackdoginstitute.org.au

BluePages

Comprehensive, evidence-based information about depression and its treatment (including medical, psychological and alternative therapies). BluesPages also includes interactive depression and anxiety quizzes, descriptions of the experience and symptoms of depression, a relaxation download, and extensive resources for help. Participation is free and anonymous.

www.bluepages.anu.edu.au

Bullying. No Way!

A site dedicated to bring schools and communities together to stamp out bullying. You can register your school for the National Day against Bullying and Violence. A great place to find the latest news about conferences and get up-to-date resources to deal with bullying in a school or community environment.

http://bullyingnoway.gov.au

e-couch

E-hub's latest interactive self-help programme includes modules for social anxiety, generalised anxiety and depression. It provides self-help training drawn from cognitive, behavioural and interpersonal therapies, as well as relaxation and exercise. Participation is free and anonymous.

www.ecouch.anu.edu.au

Headspace

Go to the website to find information, support and help near you. The National Youth Mental Health Foundation offers a comprehensive website and one-stop-shop services that are youth-specific and therefore youth-friendly. Headspace employs a range of different health workers and programmes with a focus on the needs of young people. These include, GPs, psychologists, alcohol and drug workers, as well as education and employment programs.

www.headspace.org.au

itsallright

itsallright.org is SANE's website for young people with a parent or friend affected by mental illness. Read the diaries of four teenagers, based on real stories, as they deal with the challenge of living with mental illness in their families.

www.itsallright.org

Kids Help Line

Kids Help Line offers free, confidential 24-hour telephone counselling services for 5–25-year-olds in Australia. You can email a counsellor or chat to one online at any time.

Telephone: 1800 55 1800 (free call from land line)

www.kidshelpline.com.au

Lifeline

Lifeline is a 24-hour phone counselling service.

Telephone: 13 11 14

www.lifeline.org.au

The Lifeline National Service Finder

This is a comprehensive online national database of low-cost or free health and community services offered throughout Australia. The service gives you the opportunity to look for providers in your local area.

https://lifeline.serviceseeker.com.au

MindMatters

MindMatters is about young people, their health and wellbeing. It helps schools to support young people to achieve their goals, build relationships and cope with challenges.

www.mindmatters.edu.au

MoodGYM

A popular interactive program that teaches cognitive-behaviour therapy skills for preventing and coping with depression. MoodGYM has been extensively researched and its effectiveness has been demonstrated in randomised controlled trials. Participation is free and anonymous.

www.moodgym.anu.edu.au

Orygen Youth Health

Orygen Youth Health aims to ensure that young people are able to access high-quality mental health, and drug and alcohol services provided in friendly, accessible environments.

www.oyh.org.au

Racism. No Way

Many schools, students and teachers have already demonstrated their commitment to countering racism through their involvement in developing and implementing anti-racism education initiatives.

By recording your name and comment here, you can demonstrate your support to the goals and principles of anti-racism education and eliminating racism in Australian schools and society.

www.racismnoway.com.au/get-involved/pledge-support.html

ReachOut

ReachOut.com is a web-based service that aims to inspire young people to help themselves through tough times. The ReachOut.com site has fact sheets and personal stories about a wide range of health and lifestyle issues, as well as profiles of famous people, an e-newsletter and a database where you can look for help in your area. ReachOut.com is an initiative of the Inspire Foundation.

www.reachout.com

SANE Australia

SANE Australia is a national charity helping Australians affected by mental illness lead a better life - through campaigning, education and research. SANE conducts innovative programmes and campaigns to improve the lives of people living with mental illness, their family and friends. It also operates a busy Helpline and website, which have thousands of contacts each year from around Australia.

Telephone: 1800 18 SANE (7263)

www.sane.org

Somazone

Somazone is a website that was developed by young people for young people, with the assistance of the Australian Drug Foundation (ADF). The website focuses on health and lifestyle issues such as mental health, drug use, relationships and body image, with fact sheets, personal stories and advice on where to get help.

www.adf.org.au

WhatWorks4U

This website enables young people to share what treatments have worked for their mental health difficulties and learn what treatments other young people have reported as helpful. WhatWorks4u hopes to increase awareness of treatment options and inform treatment decisions based on what has worked for similar young people. Over 500 young people have shared their experience.

http://whatworks4u.org

UNITED KINGDOM
Anti-Bullying Alliance

www.anti-bullyingalliance.org.uk

Ditch the Label: Anti-Bullying Charity

www.ditchthelabel.org

Bullying UK: Bullying Advice

www.bullying.co.uk

Bullies Out – Anti-Bullying Training, Awareness and Support

https://bulliesout.com

Kidscape: Preventing Bullying, Protecting Children

www.kidscape.org.uk

National Bullying Helpline

www.nationalbullyinghelpline.co.uk

Cybersmile – Cyberbullying

www.cybersmile.org

Stonewall – LGBT Charity

www.stonewall.org.uk

About the Authors

CATHERINE THORNTON
Psychologist, school counsellor

Cathie has been a registered psychologist for over 15 years and holds a Master's Degree in Educational and Developmental Psychology. Cathie's research thesis explored bullying in schools and how schools could develop a tailored approach to anti-bulling programmes. For the past eight years Cathie has been employed as a school psychologist working with parents, students, and teachers from Early Learning (aged 3) to Year 12 (aged 18). Her professional interests include psychometric assessment, evidence-based academic intervention and the identification of what constitutes a thriving and positive school climate. Away from work, Cathie likes to spend time with her family, growing vegetables and trying new recipes.

MICHAEL PANCKRIDGE
Teacher, author

Michael has been a teacher for a number of years. He is currently working in an independent co-educational middle school, spanning Years 4–8. He began writing around 15 years ago and is the author of over 30 children's books covering a wide range of topics – most notably sport, but more recently, books that have mystery- and thriller-style plots. In his free time Michael enjoys spending time with his daughters, watching sport, running and reading.